DATE DUE

AG 21 '92		
AP 23 '93		
JE 1 1 '93		
NO 5 93		
AG 18 '94		
MR 14 86		

DEMCO 38-296

College Degrees by Mail

100 Good Schools that Offer Bachelor's, Master's, Doctorates and Law Degrees by Home Study

John Bear, Ph.D.

1☉ Ten Speed Press

Ten Speed Press
Box 7123
Berkeley, CA 94707

Text and cover design by Fifth Street Design, Berkeley, California.

Library of Congress Cataloging-in-Publication Data

Bear, John, 1938-
    College degrees by mail : 100 good schools that offer bachelor's,
master's, doctorates, and law degrees by home study / John Bear.
        p. cm.
    Includes index.
    ISBN 0-89815-379-4
    Correspondence schools and courses—United States—Directories.
2. Degrees, Academic—United States—Directories. I. Title.
LC901.B35 1990
374'.473—dc20   90-47097
                                                      CIP

        3   4   5 — 95 94 93 92 91

Printed in the United States of America

Dedication

For Tanya Pozerycki, dilligent researcher, tireless organizer, and youngest daughter, without whose help you would not be reading this now, because the book would have come out a year later. And, as always, for Marina.

Table of Contents

Appendices

Introduction

Four Essential Facts and Assumptions

HERE ARE THE FOUR BASIC ASSUMPTIONS upon which this book is built. You already know the first, you probably know the second, you probably don't know the third, and the fourth is the reason to buy this book.

There is often no connection whatsoever between ability and degrees.

There are extremely talented and capable people who never went to college for a single day. And, as everyone knows, some of the most incompetent boobs on our planet have degrees from prestigious universities.

A degree is often more useful than a good education or valuable skills in your field.

You may be the best business manager, teacher, or pilot in three counties, but if you don't have a piece of imitation parchment that certifies you as an Associate, Bachelor, Master, or Doctor, you are somehow perceived as less worthy, and are often denied the better jobs and higher salaries that go to degree-holders, regardless of their competence.

It is easier than it ever has been to earn a degree.

Since the mid-1970s, there has been a virtual explosion in what is now called "alternative" or "nontraditional" or "external" or "off-campus" education—ways and means of getting an education, or a degree (or both, if you wish) without sitting in classrooms day after day, year after year.

But it is not always easy to find the right school.

Many of the good schools never advertise or promote themselves, either because they don't know how or because they think it unseemly. And most of the bad schools, the illegal or barely legal diploma mills, advertise all the time in national newspapers and magazines.

Let this book be your guide, your starting point, and your road map. Of course, it will require effort on your part to end up with the degree you want. I think it is safe to say that if you cannot find what you are looking for or hoping for in this book, it probably doesn't exist.

College Degrees by Mail
The Two Ideas that Make It All Possible

THERE ARE TWO VERY CLEVER IDEAS that make it possible to earn good, usable college degrees by mail. Surprisingly, both ideas have been around for a long, long time, although many people in the degree-granting business are just beginning to pay attention to them.

Idea Number One:
If you've already done it, you don't have to do it again.

When Aristotle arrived to train Alexander T. Great, it was clear to the old boy that his student *already* had learned a great deal, which did not have to be taught again, and so they could get on with the art of war and diplomacy. Compare that with many of today's students who "learn" the exports of Brazil and the parts of speech every year for eight consecutive years. As my mentor, Dr. Elizabeth Drews, wrote, "It is immoral to teach someone something he or she already knows."

Thankfully, more and more colleges and universities are giving credit for the things one already knows. If you learned a second language from your grandmother or out of a book or by living in another country, you'll still get credit for it. If you learned journalism by working on a newspaper, you'll get credit for it. If you learned meteorology while studying for your pilot's license, you'll get credit for it. That sort of thing. (How do you *get* that credit? Read on. That's what much of this book is about.)

Idea Number Two:
Meaningful learning can take place outside the classroom.

Abraham Lincoln studied law at night, by the fire. We have always known that learning can take place anywhere, any time, although for years, most universities have pretended that the only worthwhile learning, the only *degree-worthy* learning, takes place in classrooms and lecture halls. But now, more and more schools are not only acknowledging the learning that took place before you enrolled, they are making their own courses available in a multitude of ways, including

- ◆ courses by correspondence, or home study
- ◆ courses offered over cable television (or by videotape)
- ◆ courses through guided independent study, at your own pace
- ◆ courses offered over home computers linked to the university computer
- ◆ courses offered in your neighborhood, by schools that are actually located in another state or country.

Important Issues

College Degrees
What Are They?

A DEGREE IS A TITLE conferred by a school to show that a certain course of study has been successfully completed. A diploma is the actual document or certificate that is given to the student as evidence of the awarding of the degree. The following six kinds of degrees are awarded by college and universities in the United States.

The Associate's degree

The Associate's degree is a relatively recent development, reflecting the tremendous growth of two-year community colleges (which is the new and presumably more respectable name for what used to be known as junior colleges).

Since many students attend these schools for two years, but do not continue on to another school for the Bachelor's degree, a need was felt for a degree to be awarded at the end of these two years of full-time study (or their equivalent by nontraditional means). More than two thousand two-year schools now award the Associate's degree, and a small but growing number of four-year schools also award them to students who leave after two years.

The two most common Associate's degrees are the A.A. (Associate of Arts) and the A.S. (Associate of Science). But more than one hundred other titles have been devised, ranging from the A.M.E. (Associate of Mechanical Engineering) to the A.D.T. (Associate of Dance Therapy).

An Associate's degree typically requires sixty to sixty-four semester hours of credit, which, in a traditional program, normally takes two academic years (four semesters, or six quarters) to complete.

The Bachelor's degree

Most places in the world, the Bachelor's is the first university degree earned. (The Associate's is little used outside the United States.) The traditional Bachelor's degree in America is widely believed to require four years of full-time study (120 to 128 semester units), although a rather alarming report in 1990 revealed that the average time is closer to six years! But through non-traditional approaches, some people with a good deal of prior learning have earned Bachelor's degrees in as short a time as two or three months.

More than three hundred different Bachelor's degree titles have been used in the last hundred years, but the great majority of the million-plus Bachelor's degrees awarded in the United States each year are either the B.A. (Bachelor of Arts) or the B.S. (Bachelor of Science), sometimes with additional letters to indicate the field (e.g., B.S.E.E. for electrical engineering, B.A.B.A. for business administration, and so on). Other common Bachelor's degree titles include the B.B.A. (business administration), B.Mus. (music), B.Ed. (education), and B.Eng.

(engineering). Some nontraditional schools or programs award their own degrees: B.G.S. (general studies), B.I.S. (independent studies), B.L.S. (liberal studies) and so on. (Incidentally, in the late nineteenth century, educators felt that the title of "Bachelor" was inappropriate for young ladies, so some schools awarded female graduates titles such as Mistress of Arts or Maid of Science.)

The Master's degree

The traditional Master's degree requires one to two years of on-campus work after the Bachelor's. Some nontraditional Master's degrees may be earned entirely through nonresident study, while others require anywhere from a few days to a few weeks on campus.

There are several philosophical approaches to the Master's degree. Some schools regard it as a sort of advanced Bachelor's, requiring only the completion of one to two years of advanced-level studies and courses. Other schools see it as a junior Doctorate, requiring creative, original research, culminating in the writing of a thesis, or original research paper. Some programs give the student the option of choosing either approach: they may choose either to take, for example, ten courses and write a thesis, or thirteen courses with no thesis, to earn the Master's degree.

Master's degree titles tend to follow closely those of Bachelor's degrees. The M.A. (Master of Arts) and M.S. (Master of Science) are by far the most common, along with the standby of American business, the M.B.A. (Master of Business Administration). Other common Master's degrees include the M.Ed. (education), M.Eng. (engineering), M.L.S. (library science), and M.J. (either journalism or jurisprudence).

The Doctorate

The academic title of "Doctor" (as distinguished from the professional and honorary titles, to be discussed shortly) is awarded for completion of an advanced course of study, culminating in a piece of original research in one's field, known as the Doctoral thesis, or dissertation.

The total elapsed time can be anywhere from three to twelve years. The trend has been for Doctorates to take longer and longer. A typical Ph.D. now takes six or seven years, not all of it necessarily spent in residence on campus, however.

Some doctoral programs permit the use of work already done (books written, symphonies composed, business plans created, etc.) as partial (or, in a few cases, full) satisfaction of the dissertation requirement. But many schools insist on all, or almost all, new work.

The most common Doctorate is the Doctor of Philosophy (Ph.D. in North America, D.Phil. in many other countries), which need have nothing to do with philosophy. It is awarded for studies in dozens of fields, ranging from chemistry to communication to agriculture. There are more than five hundred other Doctorate titles in the English language alone. After the Ph.D., the most common include the Ed.D. (education), D.B.A. (business administration), D.P.A. (public administration), D.A. (art or administration), Eng.D. (engineering), and Psy.D.

Finally, it should be mentioned that several American schools, concerned with what one called the "Doctoral glut," are reported to be seriously considering instituting a new degree, *higher* than the Doctorate, presumably requiring more years of study and a more extensive dissertation. The name "Chancellorate" has been bandied about. Indeed, the prestigious *Chronicle of Higher Education* devoted a major article to this possibility in early 1990. It may well be that holders of a Chancellorate (Ph.C.?) would not appreciably affect the job market, since most of them will be on Social Security by the time they complete this degree.

Professional degrees

Professional degrees are earned by people who intend to enter what are often called "the professions"—medicine, dentistry, law, the ministry, and so forth. In the United States, these degrees are almost always earned *after* completing a Bachelor's degree, and almost always carry the title of "Doctor" (e.g., Doctor of Medicine, Doctor of Divinity).

In many other countries, it is common to enter professional school directly from high school, in which case the first degree earned is a Bachelor's. (For instance, there is the British Bachelor of Medicine, whose holders are invariably called "Doctor," unless they have earned the advanced degree of "Doctor of Medicine." Then they insist on being called "Mister." No one ever said the British were easy to understand.)

It is still possible to earn a law degree and many theological degrees (Doctor of Divinity, Theology, Sacred Music, etc.) through home study. Let's not even think about the consequences of attempting to teach medicine or dentistry by these methods!

Honorary degrees

The honorary degree is the stepchild of the academic world, and a most curious one at that. It has no more relationship or connection with academia than bandleader Doc Severinsen has with the world of medicine. It is, purely and simply, a title that some institutions (and some scoundrels) have chosen to bestow from time to time, and for a wide variety of reasons, upon certain people. These reasons often have to do with the donation of money, or with attracting celebrities to a commencement ceremony.

The honorary Doctorate has no academic standing whatsoever, and yet, because it carries with it the same title, "Doctor," that is used for the earned degree, it has become an extremely desirable commodity for those who covet titles and the prestige they bring. For respectable universities to award the title of "Doctor" via an honorary Doctorate is as peculiar as if the Army were to award civilians the honorary title of "General"—a title the civilians could then use in their everyday life.

More than one thousand traditional colleges and universities award honorary Doctorates (anywhere from one to fifty per year, each), and a great many Bible schools, spurious schools, and degree mills hand them out with wild abandon to almost anyone willing to pay the price. And that is why we have Doctor Michael Jackson, Doctor Ed McMahon, Doctor Frank Sinatra, Doctor Ella Fitzgerald, Doctor Mr. Rogers, Doctor Captain Kangaroo, Doctor Doctor Seuss, Doctor Jane Pauley, Dr. Bob Hope, Doctor Robert Redford, Doctor Stevie Wonder, Doctor Dan Rather, and thousands of other doctors.

Checking Out Schools
Two problems, Two Questions to Ask

A DEGREE PROGRAM IS, for many people, one of the most expensive and time-consuming things they will do in their lives. And yet some people will spend more time and energy buying a refrigerator or a television set than they will selecting a school. For such people, one of two major problems may later set in.

Problem One: The school turns out to be less than wonderful

Some people enroll in a questionable school and then, when they see their alma mater exposed on *60 Minutes* or *Inside Edition*, they wail, "But I didn't know; they had such a lovely catalog."

Problem Two: There are unpleasant surprises down the road

Some people enroll in good, legitimate schools, but then they discover, to their horror, that after three years, their Bachelor's will take *another* three years because of certain requirements they were unaware of; or that the degree title on the diploma will not be the one they expected (an anguished chap wrote me that after seven years in a program, he discovered he would be getting an M.A. in Architecture, not the Master of Architecture that he wanted); or some other dreadful situation that could have been avoided by asking enough questions in advance.

Thus there are two kinds of "checking out" to do: Will the school meet my needs? And is the school legitimate?

Question One: Will it meet my needs?

You'd think people would know this before spending thousands of dollars and years of their lives. But I have had hundreds of letters from people who received very unpleasant surprises after they had enrolled, sometimes after they had graduated. It is essential that you satisfy yourself that a given school will meet your needs before you spend any money with them. Make sure you know exactly what it will cost (no hidden "graduation fees," for instance), whether your employer will accept (and perhaps pay for) your degree, whether any relevant licensing agencies will accept the work, and so on.

Question Two: Is it legitimate?

If you have any doubts, concerns, worries, or hunches about any school, whether in this book or not, you have every right to check them out. It's a buyer's market. You can ask any questions you want about accreditation, number of students, the credentials of the people in charge, what kind of campus they have (some schools with very impressive-looking catalogs are operated from mail-forwarding services), and so on. Of course they have the right not to answer, where-upon you have the right not to enroll.

The information in this book is as complete and current as I could make it. But things change: schools change their policies, bad schools get better, good schools get worse, new schools appear, old schools disappear.

For ways and means of getting more information, see appendices A and B.

State Agencies

Some states have very tough school laws, some have very weak or almost non-existent laws, and most are somewhere in between.

Some states are very helpful and candid when someone inquires about a school in that state; others are very reluctant to say anything; and in some, it depends on who happens to receive your inquiry. Here is my current file on the appropriate agency and person in each state who is concerned with the legitimacy of schools in his or her state. (I have found that virtually all of them prefer letters to phone calls.)

Alabama
Charles Saunders, Coordinator of Private
   Schools Unit
Department of Education
348 State Office Building
Montgomery, AL 36130

Alaska
Linda Low, Director for Institutional
   Authorization
Commission on Postsecondary Education
3601 C Street, #478
Anchorage, AK 99503

Arizona
Dona Marie Markley, Director, State Board
   for Private Postsecondary Education
1812 West Monroe, #214
Phoenix, AZ 85007

Arkansas
Dr. John Spraggins, Associate Director for
   Academic Affairs
Department of Higher Education
1220 West 3rd Street
Little Rock, AR 72201

California
See information on the ever-changing
   California situation in appendix E.

Colorado
Dr. Timothy Grieder, Director, Continuing
   Education and Extended Academic
   Programs
Commission on Higher Education
Colorado Heritage Center, 2nd Floor
1300 Broadway
Denver, CO 80203

Connecticut
Dr. Donald H. Winandy, Director of
   Licensure and Accreditation
Board of Governors for Higher Education
61 Woodland Street
Hartford, CT 06105

Delaware
Dr. Ervin C. Marsh, State Supervisor,
   Certification and Personnel Division
Department of Public Instruction
Townsend Building
Box 1402
Dover, DE 19901

District of Columbia
John G. Stone III, Executive Director
Educational Institution Licensure
   Commission
605 C Street N.W., #M-102
Washington, DC 20001

Florida

Dr. C. Wayne Freeberg, Executive Director
State Board of Independent Colleges and
Universities
Department of Education
Tallahassee, FL 32399

Georgia

Dr. Janie W. Smith, Coordinator, Private
College and University Standards
Department of Education
1870 Twin Towers East
Capitol Square
Atlanta, GA 30334

Hawaii

Philip Doi, Director
Office of Consumer Protection
250 South King Street
Honolulu, HI 96813

Idaho

Eldon Nelson, Supervisor of Support Services
State Board of Education
650 West State Street
Boise, ID 83720

Illinois

Dr. Kathleen Kelly, Associate Director for
Academic and Health Affairs
Illinois Board of Higher Education
500 Reisch Building
4 West Old Capital Square
Springfield, IL 62701

Indiana

Phillip H. Roush, Commissioner
Indiana Commission on Proprietary
Education
32 East Washington Street, #804
Indianapolis, IN 46204

Iowa

Dr. Robert J. Barak, Director, Academic
Affairs and Research
Board of Regents
Lucas State Office Building
Des Moines, IA 50319

Kansas

Dr. Martine Hammond, Director of Academic
Affairs
Kansas Board of Regents
Merchants National Bank Building, 14th
Floor
Topeka, KS 66612

Kentucky

Robert Summers, Executive Director
Kentucky State Board for Proprietary
Education
P.O. Box 456
Frankfort, KY 40601

Louisiana

Dr. Larry Tremblay, Coordinator of Research
and Data Analysis
Board of Regents
161 Riverside Mall
Baton Rouge, LA 70801

Maine

Frederick Douglas, Director, Higher
Education Services
Department of Education & Cultural Services
Division of Higher Education Services
State House Station, #119
Augusta, ME 04333

Maryland

Dr. Donald Stoddard, Coordinator, Academic
Affairs
State Board for Higher Education
Jeffery Building, 16 Francis Street
Annapolis, MD 21401

Massachusetts

Dr. John Weston, Academic Program Officer,
Division of Academic Affairs
Board of Regents
1 Ashburton Place, Room 1401,
McCormack Building
Boston, MA 02108

Michigan

David Hanson, Specialist, Accreditation and
Approval
Department of Education
Higher Education Management Services
P.O. Box 30008
Lansing, MI 48909

Minnesota

Dr. E. Ann Kelly, Manager of Programs
Higher Education Coordinating Board
Suite 400, Capitol Square Building, 550
 Cedar Street
St. Paul, MN 55101

Mississippi

George Carter, Executive Secretary
Board of Trustees of State Institutions of
 Higher Learning
P.O. Box 2336
Jackson, MS 39225

Missouri

Dr. Robert Jacob, Assistant Commissioner
Coordinating Board for Higher Education
101 Adams Street
Jefferson City, MO 65101

Montana

Carrol Krause, Commissioner for Higher
 Education
Montana University System
33 South Last Chance Gulch
Helena, MT 59620

Nebraska

Sue Gordon-Gessner, Executive Director
Coordinating Commission for Postsecondary
 Education
6th Floor, Capitol Building, P.O. Box 95005
Lincoln, NE 68509

Nevada

John V. Griffin, Administrator
Commission on Postsecondary Education
1000 East William, Suite 102
Carson City, NV 89710

New Hampshire

Dr. James A. Busselle, Executive Director
Postsecondary Education Commission
2½ Beacon Street
Concord, NH 03301

New Jersey

Amorita Suarez, Director
Office of Program Review, Accreditation and
 Licensure
Department of Higher Education
225 West State Street
Trenton, NJ 08625

New Mexico

Dr. Rosalie A. Bindel, Associate Executive
 Director for Academic Affairs
Commission of Higher Education
1068 Cerillos Road
Santa Fe, NM 87501

New York

Dr. Denis F. Paul, Assistant Commissioner
Division of Academic Program Review
State Education Department
Cultural Education Center, Room 5A37
Empire State Plaza
Albany, NY 12234

North Carolina

Dr. John F. Corey, Associate Vice President
 for Planning
University of North Carolina
P.O. Box 2688
Chapel Hill, NC 27515

North Dakota

Dr. Ellen Chaffee, Associate Commissioner
 for Academic Affairs
State Board of Higher Education
State Capitol Building
Bismarck, ND 58505

Ohio

Dr. Jonathan Tafel, Director, Certificates of
 Authorization and Continuing Education
Board of Regents
30 East Broad Street, #3600
Columbus, OH 43215

Oklahoma

Dr. Melvin R. Todd, Vice Chancellor for
 Academic Administration State Regents
 for Higher Education
500 Education Building, State Capitol
 Complex
Oklahoma City, OK 73105

Oregon

Dr. David A. Young, Administrator
Office of Educational Policy and Planning
Oregon Educational Coordinating
 Commission
225 Winter Street N.E.
Salem, OR 97310

Pennsylvania

Dr. Warren D. Evans, Chief, Division of
 Postsecondary Education Services
Department of Education, 9th Floor,
333 Market Street
Harrisburg, PA 17126

Rhode Island

Dr. Cynthia Ward
Associate Commissioner of Program and
 Planning
Office of Higher Education
199 Promenade Street, Suite 222
Providence, RI 02908

South Carolina

Alan S. Krech, Assistant Director for
 Planning and Special Projects
Commission on Higher Education
1429 Senate Street
Columbia, SC 29201

South Dakota

Roxie Thielen, Administrative Aide
Dept. of Education and Cultural Affairs
Richard Kneip Building, 700 Governors Drive
Pierre, SD 57501

Tennessee

Dr. George M. Roberts, Director of Licensure
Higher Education Commission
Parkway Towers, Suite 1900
404 James Robertson Parkway
Nashville, TN 37219

Texas

Dr. David T. Kelley, Director of Institutional
 Certification
Higher Education Coordinating Board
P.O. Box 12780, Capitol Station
Austin, TX 78711

Utah

Dr. Sterling R. Provost, Assistant
 Commissioner for Veterans Education
 and Proprietary Schools
Utah System of Higher Education
355 West North Temple, Suite 550
Salt Lake City, UT 84180

Vermont

Ann Turkle, Executive Director
Vermont Higher Education Council
Box 70
Hyde Park, VT 05655

Virginia

Dr. John Molnar, Library Planning and
 Institutional Approval Coordinator
State Council of Higher Education
101 North 14th Street, 9th Floor
Richmond, VA 23219

Washington

Elaine Jones, Policy Associate
Council for Postsecondary Education
908 East 5th Street
Olympia, WA 98504

West Virginia

Dr. Douglas Call, Director of Community
 Colleges and Vocational Education
Board of Regents
P.O. Box 3368
Charleston, WV 25333

Wisconsin

David R. Stucki, Executive Secretary
State Educational Approval Board
P.O. Box 7874
Madison, WI 53707

Wyoming

Lyall Hartley, Director,
 Certification/Licensure Unit
Department of Education
Hathaway Building
Cheyenne, WY 82002

Guam

William A. Kinder, Executive Director
Pacific Post-Secondary Education Council
P.O. Box 23067
G M F, Guam 96921

Puerto Rico

Ismael Ramirez-Soto, Executive Secretary
Council on Higher Education
University of Puerto Rico Station, Box F
San Juan, PR 00931

Applying to Schools

How Many Schools Should You Apply to?

There is no single answer to this question that is right for everyone. Each person will have to determine his or her own best answer. The decision should be based on the following four factors:

1. Likelihood of admission

Some schools are extremely competitive or popular and admit fewer than 10 percent of qualified applicants. Some have an "open admissions" policy and admit literally everyone who applies. Most are somewhere in between.

If your goal is to be admitted to one of the highly competitive schools (for instance, Harvard, Yale, Princeton, or Stanford), where your chances of being accepted are not high, then it is wise to apply to at least four or five schools that would be among your top choices, and to at least one "safety valve," an easier one, in case all else fails.

If you are interested in one of the good, but not world-famous, nonresident programs, your chances for acceptance are probably better than nine in ten, so you might decide to apply only to one or two.

2. Cost

There is a tremendous range of possible costs for any given degree. For instance, a respectable Ph.D. could cost around $3,000 at a good nonresident school, or more than $80,000 at a well-known university—not even taking into account the lost salary.

3. What they offer you

Shopping around for a school is a little like shopping for a new car. Many schools either have money problems or operate as profit-making businesses, and in either case, they are most eager to enroll new students. Thus it is not unreasonable to ask the schools what they can do for you. Let them know that you are a knowledgeable "shopper," and that you have this book. Do they have courses or faculty advisors in your specific field? If not, will they get them for you? How much credit will they give for prior life experience learning? How long will it take to earn the degree? Are there any scholarship or tuition reduction plans available? Does tuition have to be paid all at once, or can it be spread out over time? If factors like these are important for you, then it could pay to shop around for the best deal.

You might consider investigating at least two or three schools that appear somewhat similar, because there will surely be differences.

CAUTION: Remember that academic quality and reputation are probably the most important factors—so don't let a small financial saving be a reason to switch from a good school to a less-good school.

4. Your own time

Applying to a school can be a time-consuming process—and it costs money, too. Many schools have application fees ranging from $25 to $100. Some people get so carried away with the process of applying to school after school that they never get around to earning their degree!

Of course once you have prepared a good and detailed resume, curriculum vita, or life experience portfolio, you can use it to apply to more than one school.

Another time factor is how much of a hurry you are in. If you apply to several schools at once, the chances are good that at least one will admit you, and you can begin work promptly. If you apply to only one, and it turns you down, or you get into long delays, then it can take a month or two to go through the admission process again elsewhere.

Speeding Up the Admissions Process

The admissions process at most traditional schools is very slow; most people apply nearly a year in advance, and do not learn whether their application has been accepted for four to six months. The schools in this book will vary immensely in their policies in this regard. Some will grant conditional acceptance within a few weeks after receiving the application. ("Conditional" means that they must later verify the prior learning experiences you claim.) Others take just as long as traditional programs.

The following three factors can result in a much faster admissions process:

1. Selecting schools by admissions policy

A school's admissions policy should be stated in its catalog. Since you will find a range among schools of a few weeks to six months for a decision, the simple solution is to ask, and then apply to schools with a fast procedure.

2. Asking for speedy decisions

Some schools have formal procedures whereby you can request an early decision on your acceptance. Others do the same thing informally for those who ask. In effect what this does is put you at the top of the pile in the admissions office, so you will have the decision in, perhaps, half the usual time. Other schools use what they call a "rolling admissions" procedure, which means, in effect, that each application is considered soon after it is received instead of being held several months and considered with a large batch of others.

3. Applying pressure

As previously indicated, many schools are eager to have new students. If you make it clear to a school that you are in a hurry and that you may consider going elsewhere if you don't hear from them promptly, they will usually speed up the process. It is not unreasonable to specify a time frame. If, for instance, you are mailing in your application on September 1, you might enclose a note saying that you would like to have their decision mailed or phoned to you by October 1. (Some schools routinely telephone their acceptances, others do so if asked, some will only do so by collect call, and others will not, no matter what.)

How to Apply to a School

The basic procedure is essentially the same at all schools, traditional or nontraditional:

1. You write (or telephone) for the school's catalog, bulletin, or other literature, and admissions forms.

2. You complete the admissions forms and return them to the school, with application fee, if any.

3. You complete any other requirements the school may have (exams, transcripts, letters of recommendation, etc.).

4. The school notifies you of their decision.

It is step three that can vary tremendously from school to school. At some schools, all that is required is the admissions application. Others will require various entrance examinations to test your aptitude or knowledge level, transcripts, three or more letters of reference, a statement of financial condition, and possibly a personal interview, either on the campus or with a local representative in your area.

Happily, the majority of schools in this book have relatively simple entrance requirements. And all schools supply the materials that tell you exactly what they expect you to do in order to apply. If it is not clear, ask. If the school does not supply prompt, helpful answers, then you probably don't want to deal with them anyway. Remember, it's a buyer's market.

It is advisable, in general, *not* to send a whole bunch of stuff to a school the very first time you write to them. A short note, asking for their catalog, should suffice. You may wish to indicate your field and degree goal ("I am interested in a Master's and possibly a Doctorate in psychology") in case they have different sets of literature for different programs. It probably can do no harm to mention that you are a reader of this book; it might get you slightly prompter or more personal responses. (On the other hand, I have gotten more than a few grouchy letters from readers saying, "I told them I was a personal friend of yours, and it still took six months for an answer." Oh, dear. Well, if they hadn't said that, it might have been even longer. Or perhaps shorter. Who knows?)

The Matter of Entrance Examinations

Many nonresident degree programs, even at the Master's and Doctoral levels, do not require any entrance examinations. On the other hand, the majority of residential programs *do* require them. The main reason for this appears to be that nonresidential students do not contribute to over-crowding on the campus, so more of them can be admitted. A second reason is that nonresidential students tend to be more mature, and schools acknowledge they have the ability to decide which program is best for them.

There are, needless to say, exceptions to both reasons. If you have particular feelings about examinations—positive or negative—you will be able to find schools that meet your requirements. Do not hesitate to ask any school about their exam requirements if it is not clear from the catalog.

Bachelor's admission examinations

Most residential universities require applicants to take part or all of the ATP, or Admissions Testing Program, run by a private agency, the College Entrance Examination Board (888 7th Avenue, New York, NY 10019). The main component of the ATP is the SAT, or Scholastic Aptitude Test, which measures verbal and mathematical abilities. There are also achievement tests, testing knowledge levels in specific subject areas: biology, European history, Latin, etc. These examinations are given at centers all over North America several times each year, for modest fees, and by special arrangement in many foreign locations.

A competing private organization, ACT (American College Testing Program, P.O. Box 168, Iowa City, IA 52240), offers a similar range of entrance examinations.

The important point is that very few schools have their own exams; virtually all rely on either the ACT or the ATP.

Graduate degrees

Again, many nonresidential schools do not require any entrance examinations. When an exam is required, it is often the GRE, or Graduate Record Examination, administered by the Educational Testing Service (P.O. Box 955, Princeton, NJ 08541). The basic GRE consists of a 3½-hour aptitude test (verbal, quantitative, and analytical abilities). Some schools also require GRE subject-area exams, which are available in a variety of specific fields (chemistry, computer science, music, etc.).

Professional schools

Most law and medical schools also require a standard examination, rather than having one of their own. The MSAT (Medical School Admission Test) is given several times a year by ACT while the LSAT (Law School Admission Test) is given five times a year by ETS.

Exam preparation

There are many excellent books available at most libraries and larger bookstores on how to prepare for these various exams, complete with questions and answers. Some of these are listed in the bibliography of this book. Also, the testing agencies themselves sell literature on their tests as well as copies of previous years' examinations.

The testing agencies used to deny vigorously that either cramming or coaching could affect one's scores. In the face of overwhelming evidence to the contrary, they no longer make those claims. Some coaching services have documented score increases of 25 to 30 percent. Check the Yellow Pages or the bulletin boards on high school or college campuses.

Accreditation

ACCREDITATION IS ONE OF THE MOST COMPLEX and confusing issues in higher education. It is also one of the most misused concepts—both intentionally and unintentionally. Let me try to make some sense out of the situation.

What is accreditation?

Accreditation is *not* a government process. It is a *voluntary* process that a school may go through, to obtain a stamp of approval from one of many private, non-government-affiliated accrediting associations.

It is important to know these things about accreditation:

- It is voluntary. No school is required to be accredited.
- Some very good schools (and some very bad schools) are *not* accredited.
- Some less-than-wonderful schools *are* accredited, but not many.
- There are over one hundred accrediting agencies, some legitimate, some not.
- Accreditation is a controversial topic in higher education. The last two secretaries of education have stated in no uncertain terms that the accrediting agencies are not doing their jobs, especially with respect to "nontraditional" schools such as the ones described in this book.
- More than a few schools make accreditation claims that range from confusing to misleading to downright dishonest.
- Accreditation is not the same thing as being licensed, chartered, approved, authorized, or recognized.

The importance of accreditation

Although *legitimate* accreditation is undeniably important to both schools and students (or would-be students), this importance is undermined and confused by three factors:

1. There are no national standards for accreditation. What is accreditable in New York may not be accreditable in California, and vice versa. The demands and standards of the group that accredits schools of chemistry may be very different from groups that accredit schools of forestry. And so on.

2. Many very good schools (or departments within schools) are not accredited, either by their own choice (since accreditation is a totally voluntary and often very expensive procedure), or because they are too new (all schools were unaccredited at one time in their lives), or too experimental (many would say too innovative) for the generally conservative accreditors.

3. Many very bad schools claim to be accredited—but it is always by unrecognized, sometimes nonexistent accrediting associations, often of their own creation.

Who accredits the accreditors?

There are two agencies, one private and one governmental, that have responsibility for evaluating and approving or recognizing accrediting agencies.

The Council on Postsecondary Accreditation (known as COPA) is a nationwide nonprofit corporation, formed in 1975, to evaluate accrediting associations and award recognition to those found worthy.

Within the Department of Education is the Eligibility and Agency Evaluation Staff (EAES), which is required by law to "publish a list of nationally recognized accrediting agencies which [are determined] to be reliable . . . as to the quality of training offered." This is done as one measure of eligibility for federal financial aid programs for students.

Both agencies will supply lists of accreditors they recognize. There is considerable overlap, but there are some accreditors recognized by one and not the other.

Accreditation and the external or home study degree

One of the frequent complaints levied against the recognized accrediting agencies is that they have, in general, been slow to acknowledge the major trend to education and degrees through home study.

A few years ago, a Carnegie Commission on Higher Education analyzed the entire situation, and concluded that

> . . . as we look toward the future, it appears likely that accrediting organizations will lose their usefulness and slowly disappear. Colleges will be judged not by what some educational bureaucracy declares but by what they can do for their students. Of much greater relevance would be statistics on student satisfaction, career advancement of graduates, and data like that.

In other words, if the students at a nontraditional, nonresident university regularly produce research and dissertations that are as good as those of traditional schools or if graduates of nontraditional schools are as likely to gain admission to graduate school or high-level employment and perform satisfactorily there—then the nontraditional school is just as worthy as the traditional school.

The recognized accrediting agencies

There is one national accrediting agency and six regional accrediting associations, each with responsibility for schools in one region of the United States and its territories. Each one has the authority to accredit an entire college or university. There are also about eighty professional associations, each with authority to accredit specific departments or programs within a school. And there are at least thirty unrecognized accrediting agencies, some legitimate, most not.

Thus, it may be the case, for instance, that the North Central Association (one of the six regional associations) will accredit Dolas University. When this happens, the entire school is accredited, and all its degrees may be called accredited degrees, or more accurately, degrees from an accredited institution.

Or it may be the case that just the art department of Dolas University has been accredited by the relevant professional association, in this case the National Association of Schools of Art. If this happens, then only the art majors at Dolas U. can claim to have accredited degrees.

So if an accredited degree is important for you, the first question to ask is, "Has the school been accredited by the national accreditor or one of the six regional accreditors?" The next question is, "Has the department in which I am interested been accredited by its relevant professional association?"

There are some jobs (psychology and nursing are two examples) in which professional accreditation may be more important than regional accreditation. In other words, even if a school is accredited by its regional association, unless its psychology department is also accredited by the American Psychology Association, its degree will be less useful for psychology majors. (One of the persistent legends about accreditation has arisen because of these matters: The belief that Harvard is not accredited. Harvard University *is* duly accredited by its regional agency, but its psychology department—and many others—are not accredited by the relevant professional agencies.)

Each of the approved accreditors will gladly supply lists of all the schools (or departments within schools) they have accredited, and those that are candidates for accreditation. They will also answer any questions pertaining to any school's status (or lack of status) with them.

The agencies that recognize accrediting agencies

◆ Department of Education, Division of Eligibility and Agency Evaluation, Bureau of Postsecondary Education, Washington, DC 20202, (202) 245-9875
◆ Council on Postsecondary Accreditation, One Dupont Circle North, Suite 760, Washington, DC 20036, (202) 452-1433

The national accrediting agency

The only recognized agency with responsibility for schools everywhere in the U.S. is the National Home Study Council, 1601 18th Street N.W., Washington, DC 20009, (202) 234-5100. While many of the schools they accredit are vocational (truck driving, small engine repair, real estate, etc.), they are empowered to accredit academic schools offering Associates, Bachelor's, and Master's degrees, but they cannot deal with schools offering Doctorates.

The six regional accrediting agencies

There are six regional agencies, each with responsibility for dealing with all schools in the states over which they have jurisdiction.

Middle States Association of Colleges and Schools
Commission on Higher Education,
3624 Market Street
Philadelphia, PA 19104
(215) 662-5606
Delaware, District of Columbia, Maryland, New Jersey, New York, Pennsylvania, Puerto Rico, Virgin Islands.

New England Association of Schools and Colleges
15 High Street
Winchester, MA 01890
(617) 729-6762
Connecticut, Maine, Massachusetts, New Hampshire, Rhode Island, Vermont.

North Central Association of Colleges and Schools
159 Dearborn Street
Chicago, IL 60601
(800) 621-7440
Arizona, Arkansas, Colorado, Illinois, Indiana, Iowa, Kansas, Michigan, Minnesota, Missouri, Nebraska, New Mexico, North Dakota, Ohio, Oklahoma, South Dakota, West Virginia, Wisconsin, Wyoming.

Northwest Association of Schools and Colleges
7300B University Way N.E.
Seattle, WA 98105
(206) 543-0195
Alaska, Idaho, Montana, Nevada, Oregon, Utah, Washington.

Southern Association of Colleges and Schools
795 Peachtree Street N.E.
Atlanta, GA 30365
(404) 897-6125
Alabama, Florida, Georgia, Kentucky, Louisiana, Mississippi, North Carolina, South Carolina, Tennessee, Texas, Virginia.

Western Association of Schools and Colleges
Box 9990, Mills College
Oakland, CA 94613
(415) 632-5000
California, Hawaii, Guam, Trust Territory of the Pacific.

The professional accrediting agencies

There are more than eighty specialized agencies, with responsibility for accrediting programs in architecture, art, Bible education, business, chiropractic, and scores of other fields. Lists of them can be found in many standard reference books (including my own, described in appendix I), or from the two agencies that recognize accrediting agencies.

Unrecognized accrediting agencies

There are a great many accrediting agencies that are not approved or recognized either by COPA or by the Department of Education. A very small number are clearly sincere and legitimate, many others are not; none will meet the needs of a person who requires an accredited degree. Here are some of the more prominent ones:

Accrediting Commission for Specialized Colleges
The only requirement for becoming a candidate for accreditation was to mail in a check for $110.

Accrediting Commission International for Schools, Colleges and Theological Seminaries
See "International Accrediting Commission for Schools, Colleges and Theological Seminaries" in this section. After the IAC was closed down by authorities in Missouri in 1989, Dr. Reuter

retired, and turned the work over to a colleague, who juggled the words in the name and opened up one state over. All IAC schools were offered automatic accreditation by the ACI.

Alternative Institution Accrediting Association
The accreditor of several phony schools.

American Association of Accredited Colleges and Universities
An unlocatable agency, the claimed accreditor of Ben Franklin Academy.

Arizona Commission of Non-Traditional Private Postsecondary Education.
Established in the late 1970s by the proprietors of Southland University, which claimed to be a candidate for their accreditation.

Association of Career Training Schools
Their advertising to schools says: "Have your school accredited with the Association. Why? The Association Seal . . . could be worth many $ $ $ to you! It lowers sales resistance, sales costs, [and] improves image."

Commission for the Accreditation of European Non-Traditional Universities
A phony European agency.

Council for the Accreditation of Correspondence Colleges
Several questionable schools claimed their accreditation; the agency is supposed to be in Louisiana.

Council on Postsecondary Alternative Accreditation
An accreditor claimed in the literature of Western States University. Western States never responded to requests for the address of their accreditor.

Council on Postsecondary Christian Education
Unrecognized agency which accredits only schools which are a part of the World Christian Church, of which LaSalle University in Louisiana is apparently the only one.

International Accreditation Association
Nonexistent agency claimed by several phony schools.

International Accrediting Association
The address is the same as that of the Universal Life Church, an organization that awards Doctorates of all kinds to anyone making a "donation" of $5 to $100.

International Accrediting Commission for Schools, Colleges and Theological Seminaries
More than 150 schools were accredited by this organization. In 1989, the Attorney General of Missouri created a fictitious school, the "East Missouri Business College," which rented a one-room office in St. Louis, and issued a typewritten catalog, with such executives as "Peelsburi Doughboy" and "Wonarmmed Mann." Their marine biology text was *The Little Golden Book of Fishes*. Nonetheless, Dr. George Reuter, Director of the IAC, visited the school, accepted their money, and duly accredited them. The IAC was promptly enjoined from operating, slapped with a substantial fine, and Dr. Reuter decided to retire. (But the almost identical "Accrediting Commission International" [see above] immediately arose in Arkansas.)

International Association of Non-Traditional Schools
The claimed accreditor of several British degree mills; allegedly located in England.

International Commission for the Accreditation of Colleges and Universities
Established in Gaithersburg, Maryland, by a diploma mill called the United States University of America (now defunct) for the purpose of accrediting themselves.

Middle States Accrediting Board
A nonexistent accreditor, made up by Thomas University for the purpose of self-accreditation.

National Accreditation Association
In a mailing to schools, the NAA offered full accreditation by mail, with no on-site inspection required.

National Association for Private Post-Secondary Education
Some people have mistaken them for an accrediting agency, although they are a school information and referral service, sponsored by several schools.

National Association of Alternative Schools and Colleges
Western States University claimed in their literature that they had been accredited by this organization, which I have never been able to locate.

National Association of Open Campus Colleges
Nonexistent accreditor claimed by several phony schools.

National Association for Private Nontraditional Schools and Colleges
A serious but unrecognized effort to establish an accrediting agency specifically concerned with alternative schools and programs.

National Council of Schools and Colleges
Nonexistent accreditor claimed by a Louisiana degree mill.

West European Accrediting Society
Established from a mail forwarding service in Liederbach, West Germany, by the proprietors of a chain of diploma mills such as Loyola, Roosevelt, Lafayette, Southern California, and Oliver Cromwell Universities, for the purpose of accrediting themselves.

Western Association of Private Alternative Schools
One of several accrediting agencies claimed in the literature of Western States University. No address or phone number has ever been provided, despite many requests.

Western Association of Schools and Colleges
This is the name of the legitimate regional accreditor for California and points west. However it is also the name used by proprietors of several large diploma mills to accredit their own schools.

Western Council on Non-Traditional Private Post Secondary Education
Started by the proprietors of an Arizona school, apparently to accredit themselves.

Worldwide Accrediting Commission
Operated from a mail forwarding service in Cannes, France, for the purpose of accrediting various American-run degree mills.

Ways of Earning Credit

Correspondence Courses

YOU CAN TAKE COURSES BY MAIL from seventy-one colleges and universities in the U.S. and Canada, even though most of them don't offer degrees by mail. However the credit you earn from any of these seventy-one schools can be applied to your degree at those schools that *do* offer degrees through home study.

Each of the seventy-one institutions publishes a catalog or bulletin listing their available courses. Some offer just a few while others have hundreds. All of the schools (except the one in Canada) will accept students living anywhere in the United States, although some schools charge more for out-of-state students. About 80 percent accept foreign students, but all courses are offered only in English.

Nine of the schools offer courses at the undergraduate and graduate level, while the other sixty-two are undergraduate only.

There is a helpful directory that is, in effect, a master catalog to all seventy-one schools. It lists the course titles of every course at each school. The abbreviated one-line course titles are surprisingly informative: "Hist & phil of phys ed," "Fac career dev in schools," and ten thousand more.

The directory is called *The Independent Study Catalog,* and it is revised every few years by the publisher, Peterson's Publications (phone 800-338-3282).

Of course, you can also write directly to the schools. All of them will send you their catalog without charge. Many of the schools have popular subjects like psychology, business, and education, but some of the more esoteric topics may only be available at one or two schools, and this directory points you to them.

Correspondence courses range from one to six semester hours worth of credit, and can cost anywhere from less than $25 to more than $200 per semester hour. The average is around $60, so that a typical three-unit course would cost $180. Because of the wide range in costs, it pays to shop around.

A typical correspondence course will consist of from five to twenty lessons, each one requiring either a short written paper, answers to questions, or an unsupervised test graded by the instructor. There is almost always a supervised final examination. These can usually be taken anywhere in the world where a suitable proctor can be found (usually a high school or college teacher).

People who cannot go to a testing center, either because they are handicapped, live too far away, or are in prison, can usually arrange to have a test supervisor come to them. Schools can be extremely flexible. One correspondence program administrator told me he had two students—a husband and wife—working as missionaries on a remote island where they were the only people who could read and write. He allowed them to supervise each other.

Many schools set limits on how fast and how slow you can complete a correspondence course. The shortest time is generally two or three weeks, while the upper limit ranges from three months to two years. Some schools limit the number of courses you can take at one time, but most do not. Even those with limits are concerned only with their own institution. There is no cross-checking, and in theory one could take simultaneous courses from all seventy-one institutions.

The Seventy-one schools

Coding as follows:

✔ = one of the thirteen schools with the most college-level courses

G = school with graduate-level courses as well as undergraduate

♥ = school that welcomes students from outside the U.S.

♦ = school that prefers not to deal with foreign students but may do so

✗ = school that will not accept foreign students

Adams State College ♥
Extension Division
Alamosa, CO 81102
(303) 589-7671
Approximately 12 courses

Arizona State University ♥
Correspondence Study Office, ASB 112
Tempe, AZ 85287
(602) 965-6563
Approximately 90 courses

Athabasca University ✗
Student Services Office, Box 10000
Athabasca, Alberta, Canada T0G 2R0
(403) 645-6111
Approximately 125 courses, only for Canadians

Ball State University ✗
School of Continuing Education
Carmichael Hall
Muncie, IN 47306
(317) 285-1581
Approximately 80 courses

Brigham Young University ✔ G ♥ ✓
Independent Study, 206 Harmon Continuing Education Building
Provo, UT 84604
(801) 378-2868
Approximately 280 courses

Central Michigan University ♥
Office of Independent Study, Rowe Hall 125
Mt. Pleasant, MI 48859
(517) 774-7140
Approximately 70 courses

Colorado State University G ♥
Correspondence Program Coordinator
C102 Rockwell Hall
Fort Collins, CO 80523
(303) 491-5288
Approximately 40 courses
Graduate courses in adult education, grantsmanship

East Tennessee State University ♥
Department of Environmental Health
P.O. Box 22960-A
Johnson City, TN 37614
(615) 929-4462
Approximately 9 courses
All courses in environmental health, rodent control, sanitation

Eastern Kentucky University ♥
Dean of Extended Programs, Perkins 217
Richmond, KY 40475
(606) 622-2001
Approximately 45 courses

Eastern Michigan University ♦
Coordinator of Independent Study
329 Goodison Hall
Ypsilanti, MI 48197
(313) 487-1081
Approximately 12 courses

Embry-Riddle Aeronautical University
Department of Independent Studies
Daytona Beach, FL 32014
(904) 239-6397
Approximately 20 courses, half in aviation subjects

Governors State University G ♥
Independent Study by Correspondence
Stuendel Road
University Park, IL 60466
(312) 534-5000, Ext. 2121
Approximately 20 courses

Home Study International ♥
6940 Carroll Avenue
Takoma Park, MD 20912
(202) 722-6572
Approximately 70 courses

Indiana State University ♥
Director of Independent Study
Alumni Center 124
Terre Haute, IN 47809
(812) 237-2555
Approximately 60 courses

Indiana University ♥
Independent Study Program, Owen Hall
Bloomington, IN 47405
(812) 335-3693
Approximately 90 courses

Louisiana State University ✔ ♥
Office of Independent Study
Baton Rouge, LA 70803
(504) 388-3171
Approximately 160 courses

Mississippi State University ♥
Continuing Education, P.O. Drawer 5247
Mississippi State, MS 39762
(601) 325-3473
Approximately 75 courses

Murray State University ♦
Center for Continuing Education
15th at Main
Murray, KY 42071
(502) 762-4159
Approximately 35 courses
Includes animal, poultry, swine, and crop science.

New York Institute of Technology ♥ ✓
American Open University, Building 66
211 Carlton Avenue
Central Islip, NY 11722
~~(516) 348-3300~~ 800-222-6948
Approximately 130 courses. Credit by examination available. Some courses available by home computer.

Ohio University ✔ ♥
Director of Independent Study
303 Tupper Hall
Athens, OH 45701
(614) 594-6721
Approximately 185 courses

Oklahoma State University ♥
Correspondence Study Department
001P Classroom Building
Stillwater, OK 74078
(405) 624-6390
Approximately 120 courses

Oregon State System of Higher Education G ♥
Office of Independent Study
Portland State University, P.O. Box 1491
Portland, OR 97207
(800) 547-8887, Ext. 4865
Approximately 100 courses

Pennsylvania State University ✔ ♥
Director of Independent Learning
128 Mitchell Building
University Park, PA 16802
(814) 865-5403
Approximately 150 courses

Purdue University ♥ ✓
Division of Media-Based Programs
116 Stewart Center
West Lafayette, IN 47907
(317) 494-7231
Approximately 8 courses
*Courses in food service, pest control,
pharmacology.*

Roosevelt University ♥
College of Continuing Education
430 S. Michigan Avenue
Chicago, IL 60605
(312) 341-3866
Approximately 60 courses
Includes three graduate courses in psychology.

Saint Joseph's College G ♥
Continuing Education, White's Bridge Road
North Windham, ME 04062
(207) 892-6766
Approximately 50 courses

Savannah State College ♥
Correspondence Study Office, P.O. Box 20372
Savannah, GA 31404
(912) 356-2243
Approximately 25 courses

**Southeastern College of the Assemblies
    of God ♥**
Independent Study by Correspondence
1000 Longfellow Boulevard
Lakeland, FL 33801
(813) 665-4404
Approximately 40 courses, mostly in religious
subjects

Southern Illinois University ♥
Division of Continuing Education
Washington Square C
Carbondale, IL 62901
(618) 536-7751
Approximately 14 courses

Southwest Texas State University ♥
Correspondence and Extension Studies
118 Medina Hall
San Marcos, TX 78666
(512) 245-2322
Approximately 40 courses

Texas Tech University G ♥
Continuing Education, P.O. Box 4110
Lubbock, TX 79409
(806) 742-1513
Approximately 90 courses

University of Alabama ✔ ♥
Independent Study Department, P.O. Box 2967
University, AL 35486
(205) 348-7642
Approximately 175 courses

University of Alaska ♥
Correspondence Study, 115 Eielson Building
403 Salcha Street
Fairbanks, AK 99701
(907) 474-7222
Approximately 65 courses

University of Arizona ♥
Continuing Education, Babcock Building
Suite 1201, 1717 E. Speedway
Tucson, AZ 85719
(602) 621-3021
Approximately 110 courses

University of Arkansas ♥
Department of Independent Study
2 University Center
Fayetteville, AR 72701
(501) 575-3647
Approximately 120 courses

University of California Extension ✔ ♥
Independent Study, 2223 Fulton Street
Berkeley, CA 94720
(415) 642-4124 510-642-4111
Approximately 200 courses

University of Colorado ♥
Division of Continuing Education
Campus Box 178
Boulder, CO 80309
(303) 492-5145
Approximately 85 courses

University of Florida ♥ ✓
Department of Independent Study
by Correspondence
1938 West University Avenue, Room 1
Gainesville, FL 32603
(904) 392-1711
Approximately 115 courses

University of Georgia ♥
Center for Continuing Education
1197 South Lumpkin Street
Athens, GA 30602
(404) 542-3243
Approximately 130 courses

University of Idaho ♥
Correspondence Study in Idaho
Continuing Education Building, Room 116
Moscow, ID 83843
(208) 885-6641
Approximately 100 courses

University of Illinois ♦ ✓
Guided Individual Study, 1046 Illini Hall
725 S. Wright Street
Champaign, IL 61820
(217) 333-1321
Approximately 140 courses

University of Iowa ✔ G ♥
Center for Credit Programs
W400 Seashore Hall
Iowa City, IA 52242
(319) 353-4963
Approximately 140 courses

University of Kansas ♥
Independent Study
Continuing Education Building
Lawrence, KS 66045
(913) 864-4792
Approximately 120 courses

University of Kentucky ♦
Independent Studies, Frazee Hall, Room 1
Lexington, KY 40506
(606) 257-3466
Approximately 125 courses

University of Michigan ♥
Department of Independent Study
200 Hill Street
Ann Arbor, MI 48104
(313) 764-5306
Approximately 30 courses

University of Minnesota ✔ ♥
Independent Study, 45 Wesbrook Hall
77 Pleasant Street S.E.
Minneapolis, MN 55455
(612) 373-3803
Approximately 265 courses

University of Mississippi ♥
Department of Independent Study
Division of Continuing Education
University, MS 38677
(601) 232-7313
Approximately 135 courses
*Offers noncredit French and German for Ph.D.
candidates.*

University of Missouri G ♥
Center for Independent Study
400 Hitt Street
Columbia, MO 65211
(314) 882-6431
Approximately 120 courses

University of Nebraska ♥
269 Nebraska Center for Continuing Education
33rd and Holdrege
Lincoln, NE 68583
(402) 472-1926
Approximately 75 courses

University of Nevada ♥
Independent Study Department, Room 333
College Inn, 1001 S. Virginia Street
Reno, NV 89557
(702) 784-4652
Approximately 65 courses

University of New Mexico ♥
Independent Study through Correspondence
1634 University Boulevard N.E.
Albuquerque, NM 87131
(505) 277-2931
Approximately 40 courses

University of North Carolina ✔ ♥
Independent Study
201 Abernethy Hall 002A
Chapel Hill, NC 27514
(919) 962-1106
Approximately 160 courses

University of North Dakota ✘
Department of Correspondence Study
Box 8277, University Station
Grand Forks, ND 58202
(701) 777-3044
Approximately 90 courses

University of Northern Colorado G ♥
Frasier Hall, Room 11
Greeley, CO 80639
(303) 351-2944
Approximately 16 courses

University of Northern Iowa ♥
Coordinator of Credit Programs
144 Gilchrist
Cedar Falls, IA 50614
(319) 273-2121
Approximately 55 courses

University of Oklahoma ✔ ♥
Independent Study Department
1700 Asp Avenue, Room B-1
Norman, OK 73037
(405) 325-1921
Approximately 200 courses

University of South Carolina ♥
Correspondence Study
915 Gregg Street
Columbia, SC 29208
(803) 777-2188
Approximately 130 courses

University of South Dakota ♥
126 Center for Continuing Education
414 East Clark
Vermillion, SD 57069
(605) 677-5281
Approximately 95 courses

University of Southern Mississippi ♥
Department of Independent Study
P.O. Box 5056, Southern Station
Hattiesburg, MS 39406
(601) 266-4860
Approximately 90 courses

University of Tennessee ✔ ♥ ✔
Center for Extended Learning
420 Communications Building
Knoxville, TN 37996
(615) 974-5134
Approximately 180 courses
Many noncredit courses in pharmacology, creative writing, Bible study.

University of Texas ♥
Correspondence Study
Education Annex F38, P.O. Box 7700
Austin, TX 78713
(512) 471-5616
Approximately 100 courses

University of Utah ♥ ✓
Division of Continuing Education
1152 Annex Building
Salt Lake City, UT 84112
(801) 581-6485
Approximately 140 courses

University of Washington ♥
University Extension—Distance Learning
GH-23, 5001 25th Avenue N.E., Room 109
Seattle, WA 98195
(206) 543-2350
Approximately 130 courses
Many foreign language courses.

University of Wisconsin ✔ ♥
University of Wisconsin—Extension
432 North Lake Street
Madison, WI 53706
(608) 263-2055
Approximately 195 courses
Many foreign language courses.

University of Wyoming ♥
Correspondence Study Department
Box 3294, University Station
Laramie, WY 82071
(307) 766-5631
Approximately 100 courses

Utah State University ♥
Independent Study Division
Eccles Conference Center
Logan, UT 84322
(801) 750-2131
Approximately 100 courses

Washington State University ♥
Independent Study, 208 Van Doren Hall
Pullman, WA 99164
(509) 335-3557
Approximately 100 courses

Weber State College ♥
Division of Continuing Education
3750 Harrison Boulevard
Ogden, UT 84408
(801) 626-6600
Approximately 60 courses

Western Illinois University ♦
Independent Study Program, 318 Sherman Hall
West Adams Road
Macomb, IL 61455
(309) 298-2496
Approximately 70 courses

Western Michigan University ♦
Self-Instructional Programs, Ellworth Hall
Room B-102, West Michigan Avenue
Kalamazoo, MI 49008
(616) 383-0788
Approximately 75 courses

Western Oregon State College
Open Learning for the Fire Service Program
Division of Continuing Education
Monmouth, OR 97361
(503) 838-1220, Ext. 483
23 courses, more than half in fire service topics

Western Washington University ♦
Independent Study, Old Main 400
Bellingham, WA 98225
(206) 676-3320
Approximately 40 courses

Equivalency Examinations

MOST OF THE SCHOOLS IN THIS BOOK would agree that if you have knowledge of an academic field, then you should get credit for that knowledge, regardless of how or where you acquired the knowledge. The simplest and fairest way (but by no means the only way) of assessing that knowledge is through an examination.

More than two thousand colleges and universities in the United States and Canada award credit toward their Bachelor's degrees (and, in a few cases, Master's and Doctorates) solely on the basis of passing examinations, but only a handful will give most or all the credit for a degree on the basis of exams.

Many of the exams are designed to be equivalent to the final exam in a typical college class, and the assumption is that if you score high enough, you get the same amount of credit you would have gotten by taking the class—or, in some cases, a good deal more.

While there are many sources of equivalency exams, including a trend toward schools developing their own, two independent national agencies are dominant in this field. They offer exams known as CLEP and PEP.

CLEP and PEP

CLEP (the College-Level Examination Program) and PEP (the Proficiency Examination Program) administer more than seventy-five exams. They are given at hundreds of testing centers all over North America and, by special arrangement, many of them can be administered almost anywhere in the world.

CLEP is offered by the College Entrance Examination Board, known as "the College Board" (CN 6600, Princeton, NJ 08541-6600). Military personnel who want to take CLEP should see their education officer or write DANTES, CN, Princeton, NJ 08541.

PEP is offered in the state of New York by the Regents External Degree—College Proficiency Programs (Cultural Education Center, Albany, NY 12230), and everywhere else by the American College Testing Program (P.O. Box 168, Iowa City, IA 52243).

Many of the tests offered by CLEP are available in two versions: multiple-choice questions only, or multiple choice plus an essay. Some colleges require applicants to take both parts, others just the multiple choice. There are five general exams, each ninety minutes long, and multiple choice only, except English, which has the option of a forty-five-minute multiple choice and a forty-five-minute composition.

CLEP offers thirty subject-area exams, each of them ninety minutes of multiple-choice questions, with the option of an additional ninety minutes for writing an essay. The cost is around $30 per test.

PEP offers forty-three subject-area exams, most of them three hours long, but a few are four hours. The fees range from $40 to $125 per exam.

Each college or university sets its own standards for passing grades, and decides for itself how much credit to give for each exam. Both of these factors can vary substantially from school to school. For instance, the PEP test in anatomy and physiology is a three-hour multiple-choice test. Hundreds of schools give credit for passing this exam. Here, for instance, are three of them:

- ◆ Central Virginia Community College requires a score of 45 (out of 80), and awards nine credit hours for passing.
- ◆ Edinboro University in Pennsylvania requires a score of 50 to pass, and awards six credit hours for the same exam.
- ◆ Concordia College in New York requires a score of 47, but awards only three credit hours.

Similar situations prevail on most of the exams. There is no predictability or consistency within a given school. For instance, at the University of South Florida, a three-hour multiple-choice test in maternal nursing is worth eighteen units while a three-hour multiple-choice test in psychiatric nursing is worth only nine units.

So, with dozens of standard exams available, and more than two thousand schools offering credit, it pays to shop around a little and select both the school and the exams where you will get the most credit.

CLEP exams are offered in five general subject areas, which are

- ◆ Social Science and History
- ◆ English Composition
- ◆ Humanities
- ◆ Mathematics
- ◆ Natural Science

Specific-subject area exams are offered in the following fields:

- ◆ American Government
- ◆ American History I and II
- ◆ Educational Psychology
- ◆ General Psychology
- ◆ Human Growth and Development
- ◆ Introductory Marketing
- ◆ Introductory Macroeconomics
- ◆ Introductory Sociology
- ◆ Western Civilization I and II
- ◆ French I and II
- ◆ German I and II
- ◆ Spanish I and II
- ◆ American Literature
  College Composition
- ◆ Analysis and Interpretation
- ◆ English Literature
- ◆ Freshman English
- ◆ Trigonometry
- ◆ Algebra and Trigonometry
- ◆ General Biology
- ◆ General Chemistry
- ◆ Computers and Data Processing
- ◆ Introduction to Management
- ◆ Introductory Accounting
- ◆ Introductory Business Law
- ◆ Calculus and Elementary Functions
- ◆ College Algebra

PEP exams are offered in these fields:

- ◆ Abnormal Psychology
- ◆ Anatomy and Physiology
- ◆ Earth Science
- ◆ Foundations of Gerontology
- ◆ Microbiology
- ◆ Physical Geology
- ◆ Statistics
- ◆ Federal Income Taxation
- ◆ Business Policy
- ◆ Accounting I and II
- ◆ Cost Accounting
- ◆ Auditing
- ◆ Advanced Accounting
- ◆ Intermediate Business Law
- ◆ Corporate Finance
- ◆ Principles of Management
- ◆ Organizational Behavior
- ◆ Personnel Administration

- Labor Relations
- Marketing
- Management, Human Resources
- Production/Operations Management

- Fundamentals of Nursing (and 15 more nursing exams)
- Educational Psychology
- Reading Instruction
- Remedial Reading

How exams are scored

CLEP exams are scored on a scale of either 20 to 80 or 200 to 800. This is done to maintain the fiction that no score can have any intrinsic meaning. It is not obvious, for example, whether a score of 514 is good or bad. But any college-bound high school senior in America can tell you that 400 is pretty bad, 500 is OK, 600 is good, and 700 is great. Still, each college sets its own minimum score for which they will give credit, and in many cases all that is necessary is to be in the upper half of those taking the test.

PEP gives standard numerical or letter grades for its tests.

Anywhere from 1⅔ to 6 credits may be earned for each hour of testing. For example, the five basic CLEP tests (ninety minutes of multiple choice questions each) are worth anywhere from eight to thirty semester units, depending on the school. Thus it is possible to complete the equivalent of an entire year of college—thirty semester units—in two days, by taking and passing these five tests.

CLEP tests are given over a two-day period once each month at more than one thousand centers, most of them on college or university campuses. PEP tests are given for two consecutive days on a variable schedule in about one hundred locations, nationwide.

Persons living more than 150 miles from a test center may make special arrangements for the test to be given nearer home. There is a modest charge for this service. And for those in a big hurry, the CLEP tests are given twice each week in Washington, D.C.

There is no stigma attached to poor performance on these tests. In fact, if you wish, you may have the scores reported only to you, so that no one but you and the computer will know how you did. Then, if your scores are high enough, you can have them sent on to the schools of your choice. CLEP allows exams to be taken every six months; you can take the same PEP exam twice in any twelve-month period.

How hard are these exams?

This is, of course, an extremely subjective question. However, I have heard from a great many readers who have attempted CLEP and PEP exams, and the most common response is "Gee, that was a lot easier than I had expected." This is especially true of more mature students. The tests are designed for eighteen-to-twenty-year-olds, and there appears to be a certain amount of knowledge of facts, as well as experience in dealing with testing situations, that people acquire in ordinary life situations as they grow older.

Preparing (or cramming) for exams

The testing agencies issue detailed syllabuses describing each test and the specific content area it covers. CLEP also sells a book that gives sample questions and answers from each examination.

At least four educational publishers have produced series of books on how to prepare for such exams, often with full-length sample tests. These can be found in the reference section of any good bookstore or library.

For years, the testing agencies vigorously fought the idea of letting test-takers take copies of the test home with them. But consumer legislation in New York has made the tests available, and a good thing, too. Every so often, someone discovers an incorrect answer, or a poorly phrased question that can have more than one correct answer, necessitating a recalculation and reissuance of scores to all the thousands of people who took that test.

In recent years, there has been much controversy over the value of cramming for examinations. Many of my counseling clients have told me they were able to pass four or five CLEP exams in a row by spending an intensive few days (or weeks) cramming for them. Although the various testing agencies used to deny that cramming can be of any value, in the last few years there have been some extremely persuasive research studies that demonstrate the effectiveness of intensive studying. These data have vindicated the claims made by people and agencies that assist students in preparing for examinations. Such services are offered in a great many places, usually in the vicinity of college campuses, by graduate students and moonlighting faculty. The best place to find them is through the classified ads in campus newspapers and on bulletin boards around the campus. In forty states, the Stanley H. Kaplan Educational Centers offer preparation for dozens of different tests, ranging from college admissions to national medical boards. Although the main method of preparation involves a good deal of classroom attendance at a center (from twenty to over one hundred hours), almost all the materials can be rented for home study. (They are at 131 West 56th Street, New York, NY 10019, (212) 977-8200; outside New York, (800) 223-1782.)

Probably the best strategy is to take a sample self-scoring test from one of the various guidebooks. If you do very well, you may wish to take the real exam right away. If you do very badly, you may conclude that credit by examination is not your cup of hemlock. And if you score anywhere in between, consider cramming on your own, or with the help of a paid tutor or tutoring service.

Other examinations

Here are some other examinations that can be used to earn substantial credit toward many non-traditional degree programs.

Graduate Record Examination   The GRE is administered by the Educational Testing Service (P.O. Box 955, Princeton, NJ 08541, (212) 966-5853) and is given at nationwide locations four times each year. There is one general aptitude test and a series of advanced tests designed to test knowledge that would ordinarily be gained by a Bachelor's degree holder in a given field. The exams are available in the fields of biology, chemistry, computer science, economics, education, engineering, French, geography, geology, German, history, English literature, mathematics, music, philosophy, physics, political science, psychology, sociology, and Spanish.

Schools vary widely in how much credit they will give for each GRE. The range is from none at all to thirty semester units in the case of Regents College of the University of the State of New York.

I once met a National Guard sergeant who had crammed for, taken, and passed three GRE exams in a row, thereby earning ninety semester units in nine hours of testing. Then he took the five basic CLEP exams in two days, and earned thirty more units, which was enough to earn an accredited Bachelor's degree, start to finish, in sixteen and a half hours, starting absolutely from scratch with no college credit.

DANTES   The Defense Activity for Non-Traditional Education Support, or DANTES, administers its own exams, as well as CLEP and PEP exams. The exams are for active military personnel, who can obtain information from their base education officers.

University End of Course Exams   Several schools offer the opportunity to earn credit for a correspondence course solely by taking (and passing) the final exam for that course. One need not be enrolled as a student in the school to do this. Two schools with especially large programs of this kind are Ohio University (Course Credit by Examination, Tupper Hall, Athens, OH 45701) and the University of North Carolina (Independent Study, Abernethy Hall 002A, Chapel Hill, NC 27514).

Advanced Placement Examinations   The College Board offers exams specifically for high-school students who wish to earn college credit while still in high school. Exams in thirteen subject areas are offered (College Board Advanced Placement Program, 888 7th Avenue, New York, NY 10106).

What if you hate exams or don't do well on them?

Don't despair. There are two other, less threatening, ways to get credit for life experience learning: special assessments and preparation of a life experience portfolio. These are discussed in the following chapter.

Credit for Life Experience Learning

THE PHILOSOPHY BEHIND CREDIT for life experience learning can be expressed very simply: Academic credit is given for what you know, without regard for how, when, or where the learning was acquired.

Consider a simple example. Quite a few colleges and universities offer credit for courses in typewriting. For instance, at Western Illinois University, Business Education 261 is a basic typing class. Anyone who takes and passes that class is given three units of credit.

Advocates of credit for life experience learning say: "If you know how to type, regardless of how and where you learned, or even if you taught yourself at the age of nine, you should still get those same three units of credit, once you demonstrate that you have the same skill level as a person who passes Business Education 261."

Of course, not all learning can be converted into college credit. But many people are surprised to discover how much of what they already know is, in fact, creditworthy. With thousands of colleges offering hundreds of thousands of courses, it is a rare subject, indeed, that someone hasn't determined to be worthy of some credit. There is no guarantee that any given school will honor any given learning experience, or even accept another school's assessment for transfer purposes. Yale might not accept typing credit. But then again, often the course title sounds much more academic than the learning experience itself, as in "Business Education" for typing, "Cross-cultural Communication" for a trip to China, or "Fundamentals of Physical Education" for golf lessons.

Eight kinds of creditworthy life experience

Here are eight major classifications of life experiences that may be worth college credits, especially in nontraditional, degree-granting programs:

1. **Work.** Many of the skills necessary in paid employment are also skills that are taught in colleges and universities. These include, for instance, typing, filing, shorthand, accounting, inventory control, financial management, map reading, military strategy, welding, computer programming or operating, editing, planning, sales, real estate appraisals, and literally thousands of other skills.

2. **Homemaking.** Home maintenance, household planning and budgeting, child raising, child psychology, education, interpersonal communication, meal planning and nutrition, gourmet cooking, and much more.

3. **Volunteer work.** Community activities, political campaigns, church activities, service organizations, volunteer work in social service agencies, hospital volunteering, and so forth.

4. Noncredit learning in formal settings. Company training courses, in-service teacher training, workshops, clinics, conferences and conventions, lectures, courses on radio or television, noncredit correspondence courses, etc.

5. Travel. Study tours (organized or informal), significant vacation and business trips, living for periods in other countries or cultures, participating in activities related to subcultures or other cultures.

6. Recreational activities and hobbies. Musical skills, aviation training and skills, acting or other work in a community theater, sports, arts and crafts, fiction and nonfiction writing, public speaking, gardening, attending plays, concerts, movies, visiting museums, designing and making clothing, and many other leisure-time activities.

7. Reading, viewing, listening. Any subject area in which a person has done extensive or intensive reading and study, and for which college credit has not been granted. This category has, for instance, included viewing various series on public television.

8. Discussions with experts. A great deal of learning can come from talking to, listening to, and working with experts, whether in ancient history, carpentry, or theology. Significant, extensive, or intensive meetings with such people may also earn credit.

The most common error people make

The most common error people make when thinking about getting credit for life experience is to confuse *time spent* with *learning.* Being a regular churchgoer for thirty years is not worth any college credit in and of itself. But the regular churchgoer who can document that he or she has prepared for and taught Sunday school classes, worked with youth groups, participated in leadership programs, organized fund-raising drives, studied Latin or Greek, taken tours to the Holy Land, or even engaged in lengthy philosophical discussions with a clergyman, is likely to get credit for those experiences. Selling insurance for twenty years is worth no credit—unless you describe and document the learning that took place in areas of marketing, banking, risk management, entrepreneurial studies, etc.

It is crucial that the experiences can be documented to the satisfaction of the school. Two people could work side by side in the same laboratory for five years. One might do little more than follow instructions in running routine experiments, setting up and dismantling apparatus, and then head home. The other, with the same job title, might do extensive reading in the background of the work being done, get into discussions with supervisors, make plans and recommendations for other ways of doing the work, propose or design new kinds of apparatus, or develop hypotheses on why the results were turning out the way they were.

It is not enough just to say what you did, or to submit a short resume. The details and specifics must be documented. The two most common ways this is done are by preparing a life experience portfolio (essentially a long, well-documented, annotated resumé), or by taking an equivalency examination to demonstrate knowledge gained.

Presenting your learning: The life experience portfolio

Most schools that give credit for life experience learning require that a formal presentation be made, usually in the form of a life experience portfolio. Each school will have its own standards for the form and content of such a portfolio, and many, in fact, offer either guidelines or courses (some for credit, some not) to help the nontraditional student prepare the portfolio.

Several books on this subject have been published by the Council for Adult and Experiential Learning (10840 Little Patunxent Parkway, Columbia, MD 21044). They will send a list of current publications.

CAEL also offers a set of sample portfolios. The cost is $65 for introductory materials plus four large sample portfolios, or $80 for nine portfolios, representing seven schools. This is the sort of thing that it may be worth trying to convince a local public or community college library to acquire.

The University of the State of New York offers a most helpful guide called the *Self-Assessment and Planning Manual,* specifically geared to their Regents College programs, but useful anywhere. The cost is $8, including postage, from Regents College, Cultural Education Center, SD45, Albany, NY 12230.

Here are twenty-four other means by which people have documented life experience learning, sometimes as part of a portfolio, sometimes not:

- official commendations
- audiotapes
- slides
- course outlines
- bills of sale
- exhibitions
- programs of recitals and performances
- videotapes
- awards and honors
- mementos
- copies of speeches made
- licenses (pilot, real estate, etc.)
- certificates
- testimonials and endorsements
- interviews with others
- newspaper articles
- official job descriptions
- copies of exams taken
- military records
- samples of arts or crafts made
- samples of writing
- designs and blueprints
- works of art
- films and photographs

How life experience is turned into academic credit

It isn't easy. In a perfect world, there would be universally accepted standards, by which it would be as easy to measure the credit value in a seminar on refrigeration engineering as it is to measure the temperature inside a refrigerator. Indeed, some schools and national organizations are striving toward the creation of extensive "menus" of nontraditional experiences, such that anyone doing the same thing would get the same credit.

There continues to be progress in this direction. Many schools have come to agree, for instance, on aviation experience: a private pilot's license is worth four semester units; an instrument rating is worth six additional units; and so forth.

The American Council on Education, a private organization, regularly publishes a massive multivolume set of books, in two series: *The National Guide to Educational Credit for Training Programs* and *Guide to the Evaluation of Educational Experiences in the Armed Forces.*

Many schools use these volumes to assign credit directly, and others use them as guidelines in doing their own evaluation. A few examples will demonstrate the sort of thing that is done:

- The Red Cross nine-day training course in The Art of Helping is evaluated as worth two semester hours of social work.

- The John Hancock Mutual Life Insurance Company's internal course in technical skills for managers is worth three semester hours of business administration.
- Portland Cement Company's five-day training program in kiln optimization, whatever that may be, is worth one semester hour.
- The Professional Insurance Agents' three-week course in basic insurance is worth six semester units: three in principles of insurance and three in property and liability contract analysis.
- The army's twenty-seven-week course in ground surveillance radar repair is worth fifteen semester hours: ten of electronics and five of electrical laboratory.
- The army legal clerk training course can be worth twenty-four semester hours, including three in English, three in business law, three in management, etc.

There are hundreds of additional business and military courses that have been evaluated already, and thousands more that will be worth credit for those who have taken them, whether or not they appear in these A.C.E. volumes.

Some inspiration

There are always some people who say, "Oh, I haven't ever done anything worthy of college credit." I have yet to meet anyone with an IQ higher than room temperature who has not done at least some creditworthy things, assuming they were presented properly in a portfolio. Just to inspire you, then, here is a list of one hundred things that *could* be worth credit for life experience learning. The list could easily be ten or one hundred times as long.

- Playing tennis
- Preparing for natural childbirth
- Leading a church group
- Taking a body-building class
- Speaking French
- Selling real estate
- Studying gourmet cooking
- Reading *War and Peace*
- Building model airplanes
- Touring through Belgium
- Learning shorthand
- Starting a small business
- Navigating a small boat
- Writing a book
- Buying a Persian carpet
- Watching public television
- Decorating a home or office
- Attending a convention
- Being a counselor at camp
- Studying Spanish
- Bicycling across Greece
- Interviewing senior citizens
- Living in another culture
- Writing advertisements
- Throwing a pot
- Repairing a car
- Performing magic
- Attending art films
- Welding and soldering
- Designing and weaving a rug
- Negotiating a contract
- Editing a manuscript
- Planning a trip
- Steering a ship
- Appraising an antique
- Writing a speech
- Studying first aid or C.P.R.
- Organizing a union
- Researching international laws
- Listening to Shakespeare's plays on tape
- Designing a playground
- Planning a garden
- Devising a marketing strategy
- Reading the newspaper
- Designing a home
- Attending a seminar
- Playing the piano
- Studying a new religion
- Visiting Civil War battlegrounds
- Taking ballet lessons
- Helping a dyslexic child
- Riding a horse

- Pressing flowers
- Keeping tropical fish
- Writing public relations releases
- Writing for the local newspaper
- Running the P.T.A.
- Acting in a community theater
- Flying an airplane
- Designing a quilt
- Taking photographs
- Building a table
- Developing an inventory system
- Programming a home computer
- Helping in a political campaign
- Playing a musical instrument
- Painting a picture
- Playing political board games
- Serving on a jury
- Volunteering at the hospital
- Visiting a museum
- Attending a "great books" group
- Sewing and designing clothes
- Playing golf
- Having intensive talks with a doctor
- Teaching the banjo

- Reading the Bible
- Leading a platoon
- Learning Braille
- Operating a printing press
- Eating in an exotic restaurant
- Running a store
- Planning a balanced diet
- Reading *All and Everything*
- Learning sign language of the deaf
- Teaching Sunday School
- Training an apprentice
- Being an apprentice
- Hooking a rug
- Learning yoga
- Laying bricks
- Making a speech
- Being Dungeonmaster
- Negotiating a merger
- Developing film
- Learning calligraphy
- Applying statistics to gambling
- Doing circle dancing
- Taking care of sick animals
- Reading this book

The matter of special assessments

There is a middle ground between taking an exam and preparing a portfolio. For people whose knowledge is both extensive and in an uncommon field (or at least one for which no exams have been developed), some schools are willing to conduct special assessments for a single student. At the University of the State of New York, both for its students and for Regents Credit Bank depositors (see the section on the Credit Bank), this takes the form of an oral examination. They will find at least two experts in your field, be it Persian military history, paleontology, French poetry, or whatever. Following a three-hour oral exam, conducted at everyone's mutual convenience in Albany, New York, the examiners decide how many credits to award for that particular knowledge area.

Credit for Foreign Academic Experience

THERE ARE MANY THOUSANDS of universities, colleges, technical schools, institutes, and vocational schools all over the world whose courses are at least the equivalent of work at American universities. In principle, most universities are willing to give credit for work done at schools in other countries.

But can you imagine the task of an admissions officer faced with the student who presents an Advanced Diploma from the Wysza Szkola Inzynierska in Poland, or the degree of Gakushi from the Matsuyama Shoka Daigaku in Japan? Are these equivalent to a high school diploma, a Doctorate, or something in between?

Until 1974, the U.S. Office of Education offered the service of evaluating educational credentials earned outside the United States and translating them into approximately comparable levels of U.S. achievement. This service is no longer available from the government which has chosen, instead, to recognize some private nonprofit organizations who perform the evaluation service.

These services are used mostly by the schools themselves to evaluate applicants from abroad, or with foreign credentials, but individuals may deal with them directly, at relatively low cost.

The costs run from $60 to $150 or more, depending on the complexity of the evaluation. Some of the services are willing to deal with non-school-based experiential learning as well. The services operate quickly; less than two weeks for an evaluation is not unusual. While many schools will accept the recommendations of these services, others will not. Some schools do their own foreign evaluations.

It may be wise, therefore, to determine whether a school or schools in which you have interest will accept the recommendations of such services before you invest in them.

Typical reports from the services will give the exact U.S. equivalents of non-U.S. work, both in terms of semester units earned, and of any degrees or certificates earned. For instance, they would report that the Japanese degree of Gakushi is almost exactly equivalent to the American Bachelor's degree.

Organizations performing these services include:

Credentials Evaluation Service
P.O. Box 24040, Los Angeles, CA 90024 (213) 475-2133

Educational Credential Evaluators, Inc.
P.O. Box 17499, Milwaukee, WI 53217 (414) 964-0477

International Consultants of Delaware, Inc.
109 Barksdale Professional Center, Newark, DE 19711 (302) 737-8715
or
P.O. Box 5399, Los Alamitos, CA 90721 (213) 430-2405

Educational International
50 Morningside Drive, New York, NY 10025 (212) 662-1768

International Education Research Foundation
P.O. Box 66940, Los Angeles, CA 90066 (213) 390-6276

World Education Services
P.O. Box 745, Old Chelsea Station, New York, NY 10011 (212) 460-5644

The Credit Bank Service

MANY PEOPLE HAVE VERY COMPLICATED educational histories. They may have taken classes at several different universities and colleges, some evening or summer school classes, perhaps some company-sponsored seminars, some military training classes, and possibly a whole raft of other, informal learning experiences. They may have credits or degrees from schools that have gone out of business, or whose records were destroyed in a war or fire. When it comes time to present their educational past, it may mean assembling dozens of diverse transcripts, certificates, diplomas, job descriptions, and the like, often into a rather large and unwieldy package.

There is, happily, an ideal solution to these problems: the Regents Credit Bank, operated by the enlightened Department of Education of the state of New York, and available to people anywhere in the world.

The Regents Credit Bank is an evaluation and transcript service for people who wish to consolidate their academic records, perhaps adding credit for nonacademic career and learning experiences (primarily through equivalency examinations). The Credit Bank issues a single, widely accepted transcript on which all credit is listed in a simple, straightforward, and comprehensible form.

The Credit Bank works like a money bank, except you deposit academic credits, as they are earned, whether through local courses, correspondence courses, equivalency exams, and so forth.

Seven kinds of deposits that can be made

There are seven basic categories of learning experiences that can qualify to be "deposited" in a Credit Bank account, and of course various elements of these seven can be combined as well:

1. College courses taken either in residence or by correspondence from regionally accredited schools in the U.S., or their equivalent in other countries.

2. Scores earned on a wide range of equivalency tests, either civilian or military.

3. Military service schools and military occupational specialties that have been evaluated for credit by the American Council on Education, as described earlier.

4. Noncollege learning experiences, offered as company courses, seminars, or in-house training from many large and smaller corporations, and evaluated by the American Council on Education or the New York National Program on Noncollegiate Sponsored Instruction.

5. Pilot training licenses and certificates issued by the Federal Aviation Administration.

6. Approved nursing performance examinations.

7. Special assessment of knowledge gained from experience or independent study.

twelve semester units. And so forth, for thousands of already-evaluated nonschool learning experiences.

The first six of these have predetermined amounts of credit. The CLEP basic science exam will always be worth six semester units. Fluency in Spanish will always be worth twenty-four semester units. Xerox Corporation's course in repair of the 9400 copier will always be worth two semester units. The Army course in becoming a bandleader will always be worth

The seventh category can be extremely flexible and variable. Special assessment is a means of earning credit for things learned in the course of ordinary living or job experience. The Credit Bank assesses this learning by appointing a panel of two or more experts in the field. Except in rare cases, it is necessary to go to Albany, New York, to meet with this panel.

The panel may wish to conduct an oral, a written, or, in the case of performers, a performance examination. They may wish to inspect a portfolio of writing, art, or documentation. Following the evaluation, whatever form it may take, the panel makes its recommendations for the amount of credit to be given. This has, in practice, ranged from zero to more than eighty semester units, although the typical range for each separate assessment is probably from fifteen to thirty credits.

The Credit Bank has, for example, conducted special assessments in journalism, ceramics, Hebrew language, electronics engineering, aircraft repair and maintenance, and Japanese culture studies, among many others.

There is a relatively modest fee ($250 at this writing) to set up a Credit Bank account, which includes evaluation of prior work (except special assessments), and one year of update service. After the first year, there is a fee each time a new "deposit" of credits is made.

Work that is, for whatever reason, deemed not creditworthy may still be listed on the transcript as "noncredit work." Further, the Credit Bank will only list those traditional courses from other schools that the depositor wishes included. Thus any previous academic failures, low grades, or other embarrassments may be omitted from the Credit Bank report.

Students who enroll in the Regents College of the University of the State of New York automatically get Credit Bank service, and do not need to enroll separately.

The address is Regents Credit Bank, Regents College, University of the State of New York, Cultural Education Center, Albany, NY 12230, (518) 474-8957.

One Hundred Good Schools Offering Degrees Entirely or Almost Entirely by Home Study

INFORMATION ON ONE HUNDRED SCHOOLS follows, on the next one hundred pages. I think it is all self-explanatory.

The one important thing to bear in mind is that things change. People usually don't think of something like a university moving (but they do), or going out of business (a major college or university goes out of business at least once a month, on the average), or changing its phone numbers (all the time!), or even changing its name (like College of New Jersey becoming Princeton, Kings College becoming Columbia, Queens College becoming Rutgers, and hundreds of other examples).

If a school is listed in the next one hundred pages but you can't get in touch with them, see appendix A.

If a school is not listed in the next one hundred pages, and you want to know about them, see appendix B.

American Coastline University

Nonresident Bachelor's, Master's, and Doctorates with an emphasis on participating over electronic bulletin boards.

5000A West Esplanade, Suite #197
Metairie, LA 70006

Telephone: (504) 830-2525   Toll-free phone: —
Fax number: —   Year established: 1986

Degree levels available: Bachelor's, Master's, Doctorates
Key person: Ray Chasse, Ph.D., Academic Dean
Recognition: Unaccredited; registered with state
Ownership: Not given in literature
Residency requirement: Nonresident

Tuition:
$1,900 to $2,400 (or students can request tuition calculated at $125 per semester hour)

Fields of study or special interest:
Many fields including: science (applied, computer, agriculture, environmental), commerce and economics, community services, human services

Other information:
The brochure says that learning outcomes are more important than how the learning was obtained. The university provides a proposed degree completion learning plan to accepted students.

Learning format: Independent study and electronic learning with faculty guidance.

Students from different countries participate through computers over electronic bulletin board networks, including CompuServe, Delphi, MCI, and GEnie networks. Students leave messages in the electronic "mailbox" and receive responses within hours or days from university faculty.

There is also an electronic bulletin board operated by the university in Vienna for direct student contact. Students without access to computers work by mail.

American Coastline has established conference sites with resident directors in Brussels, Bangkok, Hong Kong, and Amsterdam.

A prospective student must have three years experience in degree concentration area.

The address in Louisiana is a mail forwarding service, which apparently forwards mail to university administrators in California.

 # American College

Degrees and credentials for life insurance people, through independent study; some with short residency in Pennsylvania.

270 Bryn Mawr Avenue
Bryn Mawr, PA 19010

Telephone: (215) 526-1000   Toll-free phone: —
Fax number: (215) 526-1310   Year established: 1927

Degree levels available: Master's, Professional Certification
Key person: Shirley Steinman, CLU, ChFC, MSM, Registrar and certification officer
Recognition: Accredited by Middle States Association
Ownership: Nonprofit
Residency requirement: None for CLU/ChFC, short for Master's

Tuition:
$2,300 for CLU and ChFC ($230 per course), $7,505 for Master's degree

Fields of study or special interest:
Professional Certification as CLU (chartered life underwriter) and ChFC (chartered financial consultant) and Master's in financial planning, financial services and management

Other information:
Courses are developed by resident faculty at American College in Bryn Mawr and taken by students from around the world. Students study independently or in classes which are sponsored by local CLU and ChFC chapters as well as other universities and professional associations. Exams are given by computer where available.

The college operates an office of student services with counselors available on weekdays to talk by phone (answer questions/give advice). The purpose is to eliminate some of the problems that arise in distance education by providing a stronger student/college relationship.

Master's degrees require short residency, along with distance study. The Master's is offered in financial services, primarily for life insurance agents.

Formerly known as the American College of Life Underwriters.

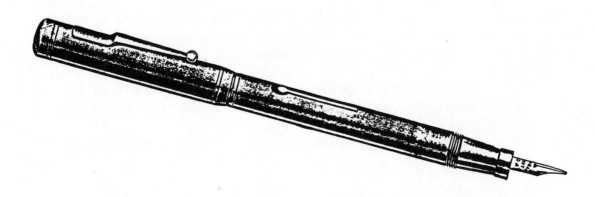

American Open University

Accredited nonresident Bachelor's degrees in business, psychology, criminal justice, and other professional areas, primarily by using a home computer.

211 Carlton Avenue
Central Ilsip, New York 11722

Telephone: (516) 348-3300   Toll-free phone: (800) 222-6948
Fax number: (516) 348-6782   Year established: 1955

Degree levels available: Bachelor's
Key person: Dr. Norma R. Talley, Academic Director
Recognition: Accredited by Middle States Association
Ownership: Nonprofit
Residency requirement: Nonresident

Tuition:
$90 per credit hour (plus extra $25 per course "communications fee") thus a possible total tuition range of about $3,000 to $12,000

Fields of study or special interest:
Bachelor of Science in business administration with a management option; in behavioral science with options in psychology, sociology, criminal justice; and community mental health. Bachelor of Professional Studies in general studies.

Other information:
The American Open University is the distance learning arm of New York Institute of Technology.

Credit is given for previous experience, demonstrated knowledge in an area, challenge exams, national exams, and course work done at the school itself. Each student is guided by a mentor who reviews assignments and provides feedback.

The program offers the same counselors, professors, coursework, and exams as given to on-campus students at the New York Institute of Technology.

All new students are required to use computer teleconferencing as mode of course delivery. Many students and one faculty member are all "on line" together, each communicating over their personal computers. However, students do not need previous knowledge of computers to take part in computer conferencing

Students have six months to finish each course they take. Each course requirement includes eight assignments and a final exam, but each professor may additionally require term papers, quizzes, a midterm, or other assignments. Exams are administered in the student's area by a school-approved proctor.

A minimum of thirty credits must be taken after enrolling at American Open University.

There is no connection with a less-than-wonderful school of the same name that has operated from Maryland, California, and Nevada.

American University of London

Nonresident degrees at all levels through an Iowa-registered school located in London.

Archway Central Hall, Archway Close
London, N193TD England

Telephone: (01) 263-2986
Fax number: —

Toll-free phone: —
Year established: 1984

Degree levels available: Associate's, Bachelor's, Master's, Doctorates, Law
Key person: Mr. S.T.H. Zaidi, Registrar
Recognition: Not accredited; state registered
Ownership: Nonprofit, independent
Residency requirement: Nonresident or residential

Tuition:
Traditional undergraduate and graduate programs: $4,000 per year. Nonresidential undergraduate and graduate programs, $2,200 per year.

Fields of study or special interest:
Liberal arts, business administration, computer science, law, natural sciences and pharmacy

Other information:
The school was originally established as the London College of Science and Technology. It operates under the laws of the states of Iowa and Utah (which register, but do not investigate schools). It has two divisions: Traditional Education Centre (residential, full time undergraduate and graduate courses which are offered in London), and the Distance Learning Centre (nonresidential).

Several Associate's degrees (science and business administration) are offered in cooperation with Arkansas State University.

For the nonresident Bachelor's degree, applicants must earn at least 75 percent of the required units elsewhere before applying.

In the nonresidential model, programs of supervised study and research are conducted under supervision of an A.U.L. appointed or approved academic advisor. Credits are earned by variety of means: independent study and research, published work, nationally approved examinations, and courses offered by the armed forces. Credit is given for prior work and experience. A thesis is required of Master's and Doctoral candidates.

 # Antioch University

One of the pioneers in U.S. higher education. Offers an accredited M.A. in many fields, with a total of two weekends on campus.

800 Livermore Street
Yellow Springs, OH 45387

Telephone: (513) 767-6322
Fax number: (513) 767-1891

Toll-free phone: —
Year established: 1852

Degree levels available: Master's
Key person: Shierry Weber Nicholsen, program director of individualized M.A. program
Recognition: Accredited by North Central Association
Ownership: Nonprofit
Residency requirement: Very short residency

Tuition:

$1,050-quarterly tuition (plus students pay about $2,600 directly to their "learning resources"—tutors, teachers, mentors, etc.

Fields of study or special interest:

Virtually any field; students choose field they want to study

Other information:

Antioch is one of the pioneers in higher education in America. Their residential campus is in Ohio, and there are regional campuses or offices in half a dozen cities in the U.S. as well as in England and Germany.

The Individualized Master of Arts requires a total of two weekends on campus: one for orientation, and one before beginning the required thesis.

There are three phases to the program:

1. Creating degree plan (design and content), done by student, Antioch faculty advisor, and two degree committee advisors chosen by student.

2. Implementing the degree plan, typically consisting of tutorials, independent studies, classes, research projects, internships, and work-related learning.

3. Completing the Master's thesis.

On occasion Antioch offers its degree in cooperation with other institutions. They have affiliations (contractual agreements) with Smithsonian Institution, Conservation Analytical Laboratory, Washington, D.C., and Rural Development Leadership Network, New York.

Average student age is thirty-six (must be at least twenty-five to apply). The majority of students are women. Up to fifteen prior learning credits may be given for either academic or experiential learning.

# Athabasca University

More than 10,000 Canadians are earning good Bachelor's degrees through this school's sophisticated home study programs.

Box 10,000
Athabasca, Alberta TOG 2RO Canada

Telephone: (403) 675-6109   Toll-free phone: —
Fax number: —   Year established: 1970

Degree levels available: Bachelor's
Key person: Kerry Joyes, Coordinator, Communication Services
Recognition: Equivalent of accredited, in Canada
Ownership: Nonprofit
Residency requirement: No residency required

Tuition:
$210 per 3 credit course, $360 per 6 credit course, $80 or $160 for challenge exams

Fields of study or special interest:
Administration, arts, general studies, nursing

Other information:
Any Canadian over the age of eighteen is eligible for admission, "regardless of previous educational experience." Non-Canadian students must be resident in Canada (that is, using a Canadian address), but may not earn degrees, and pay higher tuition.

There are four Bachelor's degrees: Administration (business administration, public administration, and organizational behavior), Arts (Canadian studies, English, French, history, psychology, and sociology), General Studies (applied studies or arts and sciences), and Nursing (post RN).

Learning is entirely at a distance, using written courses, telephone, radio, television, laboratories, workshops, computer assisted learning, audio and video tapes, and teleconference seminars (offered at more than fifty local centers, only five outside Alberta). The central component of all courses is the home study learning package which may include textbooks, workbooks, cassettes, project kits, study guides, and manuals. Each course will include various self-tests, exercises, and assignments. Exams are given at various centers throughout Alberta. Any student who lives more than one hundred kilometers from a center may use a local proctor.

Students may take a supplemental exam for each original exam taken. Final grade in a course will use whichever score was higher. Students may challenge courses by taking an exam (no supplemental exam for this).

Students are assigned a tutor for each course, to whom they have access by toll-free telephone.

Atlantic Union College

The accredited Bachelor's degree can be earned in many fields of study with a minimum of four weeks on campus.

Adult Degree Program
P.O. Box 1000
South Lancaster , MA 01561

Telephone: (617) 368-2300   Toll-free phone: (800) 282-2030
Fax number: (417) 368-2456   Year established: 1972

Degree levels available: Associate's, Bachelor's
Key person: Myron Wehtje, Co-director-ADP
Recognition: Accredited by the New England Association
Ownership: Nonprofit
Residency requirement: Very short

Tuition:
$2,340 per "unit"

Fields of study or special interest:
Many fields, including art business, behavioral science, communications, computer science, education, environmental studies, English, history, interior design, modern languages, physical education, personal ministries, religion, social work, theology, and women's studies

Other information:
Students take one "unit" a semester. A unit is a six-month study project requiring twenty hours a week. Twice a year (January and July) students are expected to spend two weeks on campus, to present a completed unit of work to professors and fellow students and plan new work, through consultation with study supervisors.

During the independent study phase, work can take a variety of approaches: practical applications, creative projects, etc. Students are expected to keep in touch with their study supervisor over the six months.

Credit equivalent to eight units will meet requirements for the Bachelor's degree. These should include one unit each in humanities, religion, science or math, and social science. Credit is given for appropriate work/life experience and documented independent study.

At least the final two units must be taken within the Adult Degree Program; thus a minimum of four weeks of residency is required to earn the Bachelor's degree.

In Massachusetts, the toll-free number is (800) 325-0099.

Bemidji State University

Accredited degrees in criminal justice, history, and social studies entirely by correspondence study.

Center for Extended Learning
1500 Birchmont Drive, N.E., #27
Bemidji, MN 56601

Telephone: (218) 755-3294
Fax number: (218) 755-4048

Toll-free phone: —
Year established: 1973

Degree levels available: Associate's, Bachelor's
Key person: Lorraine F. Cecil, Coordinator, External Studies
Recognition: Accredited by North Central Association
Ownership: Nonprofit, state
Residency requirement: No residency required

Tuition:
$40 per credit for Minnesota residents, $63 for nonresidents

Fields of study or special interest:
Associate's in criminal justice; Bachelor's in criminal justice, social studies, and history. Portions of other Bachelor's degrees may be done through external studies (psychology, English, and political science).

Other information:
Although the program was originally designed for students in northern Minnesota, there is no specific regulation governing residence, and there are some out-of-state students.

Credit toward the degree is earned through external studies courses, extension courses (in Minnesota), evening courses, and on-campus courses. The Bachelor's degree can be earned entirely through correspondence courses. Generally, the courses consist of a learning package which will include a syllabus, texts, and sometimes audio or video cassettes. The student has twelve weeks to complete each class.

Continued contact is maintained with Bemidji State in a variety of ways: by mail, telephone, exchange of cassettes, and conferences with academic advisors. As the Coordinator of External Studies put it, "unique solutions exist for unique situations." Tests may be taken on campus, or at any other location when administered by a designated test administrator.

Credit is given for experiential learning.

Brigham Young University

The Bachelor of Independent Studies is done through home study plus short periods of on-campus seminars. A nonresident Associate's in genealogy.

Department of Independent Study
349 Harman Building
Provo, UT 84602

Telephone: (801) 378-4351
Fax number: (801) 378-5278

Toll-free phone: —
Year established: 1875

Degree levels available: Associate's, Bachelor's
Key person: James M. Rawson, Director: Department of Degrees by Independent Study
Recognition: Accredited by the North Central Association
Ownership: Nonprofit, church
Residency requirement: Short residency

Tuition:
About $4,000 for degree program

Fields of study or special interest:
Bachelor of Independent Studies

Other information:
The Associate's degree is offered in genealogy entirely through correspondence study. The Bachelor of Independent Studies involves a combination of home study and on-campus seminars, and has no specific major or minor.

The Bachelor's program is divided into three phases: preparation, growth (taking courses), and closure (a research project).

Each of the five units of the program is composed of home study plus a two-week on-campus seminar. Each study area may be waived, either because of prior courses or a good score on the appropriate CLEP exam (610 or higher). (Only one study area can be waived by CLEP exam.) The total elapsed time can range from sixteen months to eight years.

British Columbia Open University

Accredited (equivalent) nonresident Bachelor's degrees in many fields for Canadian citizens.

7671 Alderbridge Way
Richmond, BC V6X 1Z9 Canada

Telephone: (604) 660-2221
Fax number: —

Toll-free phone: (800) 663-9711
Year established: 1978

Degree levels available: Bachelor's
Key person: Ian Mugridge, Principal
Recognition: Equivalent of accredited, in Canada
Ownership: Nonprofit
Residency requirement: No residency required

Tuition:
$35 to $45 per credit

Fields of study or special interest:
Administrative studies, applied science and natural resources, arts, education, health science, human service, science

Other information:
The program is only available to Canadian citizens. The university is part of the Open Learning Agency of British Columbia. It administers a provincial credit bank and offers collaborative programs in such areas as fine art, music therapy, and health science with other provincial institutions. The credit bank allows students to accumulate credit for previous college courses, other courses and programs, and experiential learning.

A course package is sent to each student at the beginning of each course. It includes a course manual, textbooks, and assignments. It may also include audio or video cassettes, lab kits, or software (for some courses the student must have access to a computer). For some courses, support programs are broadcast on the Knowledge Network television channel.

At the end of most courses, a final exam is given at exam centers throughout Canada.

They offer three types of degree programs. The Major Program requires specialization in one area. Classroom study may be required to complete the degree. The General Program requires lower level of specialization in two areas. General Studies allows the student to choose as much or little specialization as desired. In the latter two methods, work is done through "open study" at a distance.

For every course, the student is assigned a tutor. Tutors have regularly scheduled telephone consultation hours.

The university also offers graduate-level courses, but not a graduate degree program.

 # Burlington College

The accredited Bachelor's requires one week in residency, and can be completed in as short a time as six months.

95 North Avenue
Burlington, VT 05401

Telephone: (802) 862-9616   Toll-free phone: —
Fax number: —   Year established: 1972

Degree levels available: Associate's, Bachelor's
Key person: Director of Admissions
Recognition: Accredited by the New England Association
Ownership: Nonprofit, independent
Residency requirement: One week

Tuition:
About $2,000 per semester

Fields of study or special interest:
Organized degree programs in psychology, transpersonal psychology, humanities, fine arts, and feminist studies. Other subjects must be approved by Academic Review Committee. Students are encouraged to develop their own majors through the BAIM (Bachelor of Arts Individualized Major) program.

Other information:
All students must attend a one-week workshop in Burlington at the start of the program, and are encouraged but not required to attend a one-week residential session once a year. Because of the desirability of meeting from time to time with faculty advisors, students who live far from Vermont, or who cannot visit Vermont, are not encouraged.

The school prefers that an applicant already have sixty or more semester units completed at the time of enrollment.

Students are encouraged to develop their own majors, through the BAIM (BA Individualized Major) program. The program begins with a short course in contract-based learning (CBL), during which a learning contract is developed and specialists are selected. There is an academic advisor and three outside specialists who serve on their evaluation board, but the main responsibility for designing the program lies with the student.

The minimum time for degree completion is six months.

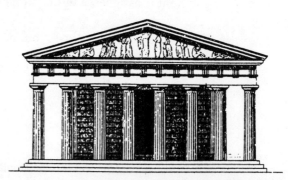

 # Caldwell College

Accredited Bachelor's degrees can be earned in various fields with only four days a year on campus.

9 Ryerson Avenue
Caldwell, NJ 07006

Telephone: (201) 228-4424   Toll-free phone: —
Fax number: —   Year established: 1939

Degree levels available: Bachelor's
Key person: Edward Clemens, Corporate Education/Adult Recruitment
Recognition: Accredited by the Middle States Association
Ownership: Nonprofit
Residency requirement: Four days per year

Tuition:
$179 per credit

Fields of study or special interest:
Business, English, foreign languages, history, psychology, religion, sociology

Other information:
The external program is designed for people twenty-three years or older. Credit is given for life experience learning, and equivalency examinations. Most of the work is done through home study, but each student is expected to spend one weekend on campus at the beginning of each new semester.

Work is completed through independent study as well as traditional academic course work. Students mail in assignments, have phone conferences with instructors, and make use of video and computer technology.

California Coast University

Bachelor's, Master's, and Doctorates in administration, engineering, education, and behavioral sciences entirely through home study.

700 North Main Street
Santa Ana, CA 92701

Telephone: (714) 547-9625   Toll-free phone: —
Fax number: —   Year established: 1974

Degree levels available: Bachelor's, Master's, Doctorates
Key person: Thomas M. Neal, Jr., President
Recognition: Not accredited; state approved
Ownership: Proprietary
Residency requirement: No Residency requirement

Tuition:
$2,225 to $3,625 for complete degree programs

Fields of study or special interest:
Administration and management, engineering, behavioral science, and education

Other information:
California Coast University was one of the first of California's nontraditional, nonresident universities. Credit is given for prior achievements and experience. Students may request "credit by experiential learning," and/or may be given the opportunity to take a challenge examination prepared and administered by the university.

Each student is assigned a faculty advisor who guides in development of an individualized study program. Each study program includes independent study as well as additional testing, writing, and research if deemed necessary.

All students develop a proposal for a topic to study which is appropriate for their major and degree level, and write a research project (or thesis or dissertation). All department heads and adjunct faculty hold degrees from traditional schools. The university operates from its own building in a Los Angeles suburb, and maintains a lending library to ensure availability of textbooks for all students throughout the world.

California Coast claims accreditation from the National Association for Private Nontraditional Schools and Colleges, an unrecognized accrediting agency.

Original name: California Western University.

[SEE APPENDIX E REGARDING THE CHANGING SITUATION IN CALIFORNIA.]

California College for Health Sciences

Accredited Master of Science in community health administration may be earned entirely through correspondence study.

222 West 24th Street
National City, CA 92050

Telephone: (619) 477-4800   Toll-free phone: (800) 221-7374
Fax number: (619) 477-4360   Year established: 1979

Degree levels available: Associate's, Master's
Key person: Chuck Sinks, President
Recognition: Accredited by the National Home Study Council
Ownership: Proprietary
Residency requirement: No residency required

Tuition:
1 credit course $165, 2 credit course $245, 3 credit course $330, 4 credit course $400; Master's requires completion of 36 semester credits, thus approximately $3,600 to $4,400

Fields of study or special interest:
Master of Science in Community Health Administration and Wellness Promotion; Associate's in applied science, certificates in wellness counseling, wellness program development, and wellness management

Other information:
The Master's program is designed particularly for those already employed in health care settings. It prepares professionals to become specialists in health promotion in private industry and education.

The core of the program is a series of correspondence courses. Texts and syllabuses are mailed to the students who complete assignments, mail them in, and have comments and corrections mailed back by the faculty.

Students are expected to complete one credit per month, so that a three-credit course should take three months, and normally *must* be completed within six months.

Students may challenge courses by completing the final exam without taking the course. Exams must be supervised by an approved proctor, and may be taken anywhere.

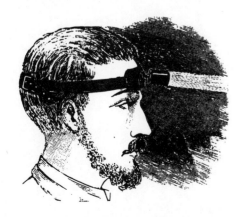

California Pacific University

Nonresident Bachelor's, Master's, and Doctorates in a very structured program.

10650 Treena Street, Room 203
San Diego, CA 92131

Telephone: (619) 695-3292
Fax number: —

Toll-free phone: —
Year established: 1976

Degree levels available: Bachelor's, Master's, Doctorates
Key person: N. Charles Dalton, Ph.D., President
Recognition: Not accredited; state approved
Ownership: Nonprofit, private
Residency requirement: No residency required

Tuition:
Master's and 12-course Bachelor's: $2,700; 18-course Bachelor's: $4,050; Ph.D.: $4,050

Fields of study or special interest:
Business administration; management and human behavior (Master's only)

Other information:
The school is "committed to the training and education of business managers and leaders in the technical, quantitative, and theoretical areas of business management (as well as in) interpersonal skills and human resource management."

Highly structured programs utilize home study delivery systems. Credit is earned through correspondence courses. Students are supplied with assignments and study guide written by university faculty to go with a textbook (which they purchase).

The Bachelor's program is designed as completion program for those who already have about two years of college. Those students take twelve courses. Students with less credit or experience take eighteen courses for the Bachelor's.

Students study one course at a time, and proceed through program course by course. Those in the twelve-course program have three years to finish; in the eighteen-course program, one has four years. Comprehensive exams can be taken locally under the supervision of a local proctor.

[SEE APPENDIX E REGARDING THE CHANGING SITUATION IN CALIFORNIA.]

California State University Dominguez Hills

Accredited M.A. in philosophy, music, art, history, or literature entirely through home study.

External Degree Program in the Humanities
1000 East Victoria Street
Carson, CA 90747

Telephone: (213) 516-3743
Fax number: (213) 516-3449

Toll-free phone: —
Year established: 1960

Degree levels available: Master's
Key person: Dr. Arthur Harshman, Program Coordinator
Recognition: Accredited by Western Association
Ownership: Nonprofit, state
Residency requirement: No residency required

Tuition:
About $120 per semester unit; minimum of 30 semester units to graduate

Fields of study or special interest:
Humanities, which includes history, literature, philosophy, music, and art

Other information:
The Master of Arts can be earned entirely through home study, primarily through a method called "parallel instruction" in which the student at home does pretty much the same thing as residential students do, in the same time frame. They simply do not attend class.

Credit is given for independent study projects, correspondence courses, and a thesis or creative project.

Students may pursue the degree entirely in one of the five areas, or by following a curriculum that includes and integrates all five areas.

Each course is accompanied by a study guide. Grading is based on written assignments. Professors guide students through courses by means of mail, telephone, and cassettes.

At least thirty semester hours are required for the degree. Eighty percent must be earned after enrolling. A full-time student can finish in one academic year.

This is an unusual opportunity to earn an accredited Master's degree nonresidentially from a major university. My wife completed her M.A. in philosophy here in 1985, at a time when we were living in a remote rural location, and she could not have earned such a degree in any other way.

Canadian School of Management

Accredited nonresident Associate's, and the equivalent of Bachelor's and Master's in management and related fields, entirely through home study.

121 Bloor Street East, Suite 1003
Toronto, Ontario M4W 3M5 Canada

Telephone: (416) 960-3805   Toll-free phone: —
Fax number: —   Year established: 1976

Degree levels available: Associate's, and equivalent of Bachelor's and Master's
Key person: George Korey, LL.M., LL.D., D.Sc.Econ., President
Recognition: Accredited by National Home Study Council
Ownership: Nonprofit, private
Residency requirement: No residency required

Tuition:

Approximately $3,600 for Associate's, $3,500 to $7,000 for Bachelor's equivalent; $6,500 for Master's equivalent

Fields of study or special interest:

Management education, administration (health services or long-term care), business administration, international management, health facility management, food service management, travel counseling

Other information:

While there are residential programs, all work can be done at a distance, through faculty-guided independent study. A faculty advisor is appointed in the geographic area where a student lives. Weekly telephone consultations are available, and a monthly teleconferencing service is offered, as well as telephone access to a library consultant in Toronto.

The School does not award Bachelor's and Master's degrees, but rather "Graduate" and "Fellow" designations, which are equivalent to Bachelor's and Master's. Students may enroll for the M.B.A. offered by City University, Seattle, and on completion of their eight distance-learning courses, also receive the "Fellow" designation from CSM. Alternatively, students may apply their CSM credits to receive the M.B.A. from the unaccredited Hawthorne University in Utah. The Union Institute (Cincinnati, Ohio) recognizes the Fellow of Business Administration award as meeting their requirements for mastery of the field in their Ph.D. program in management.

At the Associate level, CSM offers only the second year of a two-year program; at the Bachelor's level, the third and fourth years of a four-year program. The Fellow (Master's level) program consists of sixteen courses. Exemptions are made for work done at other institutions or "documented knowledge acquired through on-the-job experience." U.S. address: 1552 Hertel Avenue, Suite 210, Buffalo, NY 14216.

Central Michigan University

Off-campus accredited Bachelor's and Master's in various fields. If you can organize a large enough local group anywhere, the university will come to you.

Extended Degree Program
Rowe Hall 131
Mt. Pleasant, MI 48859

Telephone: (517) 774-3868
Fax number: —

Toll-free phone: (800) 950-1144
Year established: 1892

Degree levels available: Bachelor's, Master's
Key person: Robert Trullinger, Director, Extended Degree Programs
Recognition: Accredited by the North Central Association
Ownership: Nonprofit, state
Residency requirement: No residency required

Tuition:
$110 per credit hour for undergrads; $146 for grads

Fields of study or special interest:
Bachelor of Science in community development, administration; Master of Science in Administration; Master of Arts in community leadership or education

Other information:
Student can earn a general administration degree or specialize in health services administration or public administration.

Intensive classes are given at many locations around the U.S. All programs are operated under the sponsorship of companies, military bases, or professional organizations. In most cases, anyone may enroll, whether or not they have an association with the sponsor.

The University maintains extended degree program offices in four states (Michigan, Virginia, Hawaii, and Missouri) and program centers are located in dozens more, plus two in Alberta, Canada.

At the Bachelor's level, one semester of credit (fifteen units) can also be earned through correspondence study.

Degree programs are structured to meet needs of groups in each area, so not all courses are available at all centers. The University will consider offering a Master's program at any location where enough students can be enrolled.

For the Master's, twenty-one semester hours (of thirty-six required) must be completed through CMU. Up to ten units can come from prior learning assessment.

 # Century University

Nonresident Bachelor's, Master's and Doctorates in many fields.

2155 Louisiana Boulevard, N.E., Suite 8600
Albuquerque, NM 87110

Telephone: (505) 889-2711   Toll-free phone: —
Fax number: —   Year established: 1978

Degree levels available: Bachelor's, Master's, Doctorates
Key person: Donald Breslow, President
Recognition: Unaccredited; state-registered
Ownership: Proprietary
Residency requirement: No residency required

Tuition:
$2,495 to $3,395 for complete degree program

Fields of study or special interest:
Business and public administration, health care management, psychology, engineering, computer science, education

Other information:
While Century generally seems to satisfy its students, two things cause me concern. One is that they have claimed for years to be fully accredited, but never with a recognized agency. "Accrediting Commission International" is the successor to the International Accrediting Commission, which was closed by Missouri authorities a few years ago. And Century's catalog badly misrepresents the findings of a 1978 government study on the acceptability of nontraditional degrees.

Students spend six to twenty-four months. The programs are designed for people who have careers and want to do further work related to their career objectives. A study plan is based on occupational needs, using the workplace as place of learning.

Applicants are expected to have substantial experience in their field. Each student is assigned a faculty advisor with whom he or she develops an independent study plan. No classes are available or necessary in this model. Mastery of subject matter is proved through term papers, case studies, and work-related projects. At the Bachelor's and Master's level, exams are required on enrollment.

Century's literature mentions regional faculty centers, with advisors/mentors throughout the U.S. and in Switzerland, the Netherlands, Saudi Arabia, and Ethiopia.

In 1990, Century moved from Los Angeles to Albuquerque. Twelve of the thirty-two listed faculty have their own doctorates from Century, an unusually high percentage. While New Mexico calls its registration process "approval," according to the book *Diploma Mills: Degrees of Fraud,* no approving is done; it is simply an automatic registration process.

Charter Oak College

Accredited Associate's and Bachelor's degrees through home study at very low cost, but for New England residents only.

270 Farmington Avenue, Suite 171
Farmington, CT 06032

Telephone: (203) 677-0076
Fax number: —

Toll-free phone: (800) 842-2220 (CT only)
Year established: 1973

Degree levels available: Associate's, Bachelor's
Key person: Helen K. Giliberto, Director of Administration
Recognition: Accredited by the New England Association
Ownership: Nonprofit, state
Residency requirement: No residency required

Tuition:
About $400 total, plus an extra $150–250 per year to continue as active student

Fields of study or special interest:
Many, including business, mathematics, science and technology, behavioral sciences, human services, humanities, social sciences

Other information:
Enrollment is open only to residents of Connecticut and the other five New England states (Massachusetts, Rhode Island, New Hampshire, Vermont, and Maine). They used to accept enrollments from people anywhere in the world, but it just didn't work out satisfactorily.

One hundred twenty credits must be amassed for the Bachelor's degree, at least half of them in subjects traditionally included among the liberal arts and sciences, and thirty-six in a single subject or major area.

Credit is earned through traditional classes taken elsewhere (Charter Oak does not offer any of its own), noncollegiate instruction (such as military study), testing to prove competency/knowledge level (proficiency exams), and correspondence courses taken from other schools.

Each student submits a program proposal which becomes a learning contract when approved. Progress reports showing candidacy status are issued regularly. When all necessary credits have been accumulated, the record is reviewed by faculty to determine if the degree should be awarded.

Charter Oak's original name: Connecticut Board for State Academic Awards.

Some people have apparently attempted to abuse the "New England residents only" policy by using convenience addresses in that region. There is really no need for this, since both Thomas Edison State College and the University of the State of New York offer comparable programs. Both are described in this book.

 **City University**

Accredited nonresident Associate's, Bachelor's, and Master's through home study, optionally using a home computer to communicate with the school.

16661 Northup Way
Bellevue, WA 98008

Telephone: (206) 643-2000　　　　Toll-free phone: (800) 542-7845 (WA)
　　　　　　　　　　　　　　　　　　　　　　　　　(800) 426-5596 (elsewhere)

Fax number: —　　　　　　　　　Year established: 1973

Degree levels available: Associate's, Bachelor's, Master's
Key person: Peggy J. Arnold, Registrar
Recognition: Accredited by Northwest Association
Ownership: Nonprofit, independent
Residency requirement: No residency required

Tuition:
Five-credit undergraduate courses are $595 each (5 credits per course); 3-credit graduate courses are $486 each.

Fields of study or special interest:
Business administration and management (many specialized areas), health care administration, computer science, nursing, accounting, finance, education, and aviation management. Other fields by special arrangement.

Other information:
The degrees are offered via distance learning anywhere in the world. PLE (prior learning experience program) allows students to get credit for life experience. There is a course in portfolio preparation. The portfolio is then evaluated by a review committee to determine how many credits the student will be given (maximum of forty-five).

An instructor is assigned to each distance learner for each course. The student is given a course outline, textbook, assignments, tests, etc. Students may communicate with their instructors by mail or with computer modems over telephone lines. Courses must be finished in ten weeks. Research papers are required for most courses. Midterm and final exams are given locally by proctors.

Students with special fields of interest may request a "panel for directed study" consisting of at least one senior faculty member and an expert in the field who will work out an independent study course with the student.

City University offers programs all over the state of Washington; in Portland, Oregon; Santa Clara, California; several British Columbia locations; and in Zurich, Switzerland.

City University Los Angeles

Nonresident Bachelor's, Master's, Doctorates, and Law degrees.

3960 Wilshire Boulevard
Los Angeles, CA 90010

Telephone: (213)382-3801
Fax number: —

Toll-free phone: (800) 262-8388
Year established: 1974

Degree levels available: Bachelor's, Master's, Doctorates, Law
Key person: Dr. Henry L. N. Anderson, Chancellor
Recognition: Unaccredited, state authorized
Ownership: Nonprofit, private
Residency requirement: No residency required

Tuition:
$3,031 to $4,700 for complete degree program; Law is $2,475 per year

Fields of study or special interest:
Business administration, education, applied science, nursing, humanities, law. Graduate degrees also offered in electromedical sciences and life science/natural hygiene.

Other information:
While C.U.L.A. appears to have many satisfied students, I have been concerned for years that City University Los Angeles (there is no "of" in the name) claims to be fully accredited, although never with a recognized agency. (In the summer of 1990, literature mailed still claimed accreditation from the International Accrediting Commission, although that agency was closed by Missouri authorities in early 1989.)

The school considers itself a "finishing school" for already skilled, knowledgeable people whose studies were interrupted earlier in life. Degree programs are based on contract learning, in which a faculty member approves a plan of study. The instructional process emphasizes independent study and individual research.

There is a two-day Bachelor's "challenge exam" for persons who have completed 75 percent of the work for a Bachelor's elsewhere.

Law students qualify to take the California bar exam. This is a four-year program. Students must pass the "baby bar" after one year, then work for three more years in the program.

The catalog refers to offices and centers in many other countries, and reports that Johnny Carson, Ethel Kennedy, and Coretta Scott King are alumni of the school. (C.U.L.A. is not mentioned in the *Who's Who* biographies of these people, and I have never received replies to my inquiries to them directly.)

[SEE APPENDIX E REGARDING THE CHANGING SITUATION IN CALIFORNIA.]

Columbia Pacific University

Nonresident degrees at all levels from one of the largest schools of its kind.

1415 3rd Street
San Rafael, CA 94901

Telephone: (415) 459-1650

Fax number: (415) 459-5856

Toll-free phone: (800) 552-5522 (CA)
(800) 227-0119 (elsewhere)

Year established: 1978

Degree levels available: Bachelor's, Master's, Doctorates, Law
Key person: Richard Crews, M.D., President
Recognition: Not accredited; state approved
Ownership: Proprietary
Residency requirement: No residency required

Tuition:
Bachelor's $945/quarter; Master's $990/quarter; Doctorate $1,035/quarter, plus fees

Fields of study or special interest:
There are four schools: Arts and Sciences, Administration and Management, Health and Human Services, International Law and Business. There is a wide range of degrees within these schools.

Other information:
Columbia Pacific claims to be the largest nontraditional school of its kind, with more than five thousand students enrolled.

Students complete CPU's "core curriculum" which consists of four "projects" of directed reading, workbook exercises, essays, self-assessment, and independent study. The structure of the curriculum is the same for all, but students help shape their studies in what they are particularly interested in studying. Each student completes a major project, thesis, or dissertation.

There is a minimum enrollment time of nine months. A quarterly surcharge is added for persons who do not finish within one year.

The law degree, in international law, is for people who wish to learn more law and have a law degree, but it does not qualify one to take the California bar exam.

Columbia Pacific operates from its own office building in San Rafael, near San Francisco, and from a "retreat center" in Petaluma, California. Fifteen percent of the faculty have their own Doctorates from Columbia Pacific, which is an unusually high percentage. I served as a consultant to Columbia Pacific in its early years. I was paid in stock, which I disposed of when I became disinvolved in 1984.

[SEE APPENDIX E REGARDING THE CHANGING SITUATION IN CALIFORNIA.]

Columbia Union College

Accredited Associate's and Bachelor's in many fields, entirely through correspondence study.

7600 Flower Avenue
Takoma Park, MD 20912

Telephone: (301) 891-4165
Fax number: (301) 270-1618

Toll-free phone: —
Year established: 1904

Degree levels available: Associate's, Bachelor's
Key person: Sheila Burnette, Director of Admissions
Recognition: Accredited by Middle States Association
Ownership: Nonprofit, church
Residency requirement: No residency required for some programs

Tuition:
$117 per credit hour

Fields of study or special interest:
Associate's in general studies; Bachelor's in business administration, general studies, health care administration, respiratory therapy, religion

Other information:
In most programs, all work is done by correspondence courses. The student is sent a syllabus, textbook, and assignments. All courses require proctored exams, which may be taken anywhere.

Contact is maintained between student and instructor of each course through mail, phone, and progress evaluations. A short residency is required for the degree in health care administration (one two-week session) and respiratory therapy (two two-week sessions).

Credit is given for experiential learning when demonstrated through competency examinations. Maximum credit for this is twenty-four semester hours. Credit is also given for standard equivalency examinations or work experience after the student has earned at least twenty-four semester hours in the program.

At least thirty units must be earned after enrolling at CU (representing between eight and twelve courses.) All students must write a major paper, related to literature, science, religion, or arts or pass a comprehensive examination to qualify for graduation.

The school is operated by the Seventh-Day Adventist Church, but nonchurch members are welcome. Students may live anywhere in the world, but all work must be done in English.

Cook's Institute of Electronics Engineering

Bachelor of Science in Electronics Engineering entirely by home study.

4251 Cypress Drive
Jackson, MS 39212

Telephone: (601) 371-1351   Toll-free phone: —
Fax number: —   Year established: 1945

Degree levels available: Bachelor's
Key person: Wallace Cook, founder and director
Recognition: Unaccredited
Ownership: Proprietary
Residency requirement: No residency required

Tuition:
$5,929 to $6,538.62 depending on the payment plan, for full thirty-six-course program. Less if fewer courses are taken.

Fields of study or special interest:
Electronics engineering

Other information:
The B.S.E.E. (Bachelor of Science in Electronics Engineering) is offered entirely through home study, by completing thirty-six courses. Up to twenty-one of the thirty-six can be waived for prior schooling and experience. Students must have previous experience as an electronics technician. Cook's reviews a student's background and decides what number of courses at their school will be necessary before receiving a degree.

The school literature explains in great detail why they are not accredited (no home study engineering program is), and makes clear the distinction between their B.S.E.E. and the correspondence B.S. in Engineering Technology offered by their chief competitor, Grantham.

Wallace Cook, the owner, established this school more than forty years ago.

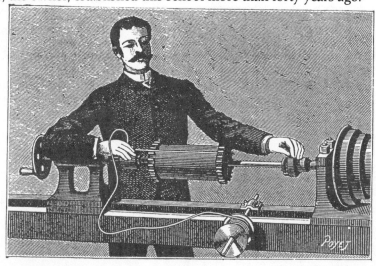

Eckerd College

Accredited Bachelor's degrees in liberal arts fields entirely through home study.

Program for Experienced Learners
4200 54th Avenue South
St. Petersburg, FL 33711

Telephone: (813) 864-8226
Fax number: (813) 866-2304

Toll-free phone: —
Year established: 1959

Degree levels available: Bachelor's
Key person: Dana E. Cozad, Director of Program for Experienced Learners
Recognition: Accredited by the Southern Association
Ownership: Nonprofit, church
Residency requirement: No residency required

Tuition:
$485 per course

Fields of study or special interest:
Many majors in liberal arts, including management, human resources, psychology, history, religion

Other information:
Home study courses are prepared by faculty members. They require no classroom participation or campus residence.

Students may enroll either in directed or independent study. Directed study means basic correspondence courses. Independent study is initiated by the student to meet special interests. The content and format of each course is determined by the supervising faculty member, and approved by the director of PEL.

Credit can be earned by examination. Credit for experiential learning is earned by taking a required course in how to document this learning. One learns how to prepare a portfolio which details what one has done. The portfolio is assessed by Eckerd faculty who determine the amount of credit to be awarded. The same course involves working out a degree plan covering the conditions that need to be met to earn the degree desired. Degree plans may also allow students to use current career experience as part of their program.

Interdisciplinary programs are also a possibility: programs tailored to individual student needs and wishes by the faculty. This may involve taking courses in various disciplines. At least nine units must be earned through Eckerd.

Eckerd was originally called Florida Presbyterian College.

Electronic University Network

Accredited Bachelor's and Master's through home study, with work done on a home computer connected by telephone to the school.

385 8th Street
San Francisco, CA 94103

Telephone: (415) 552-6000   Toll-free phone: (800) 225-3276
Fax number: —   Year established: 1983

Degree levels available: Bachelor's, Master's
Key person: Ned Davis, Vice President
Recognition: Accredited degree programs are available
Ownership: Proprietary
Residency requirement: No residency required

Tuition:
$300 to $500 per course

Fields of study or special interest:
Business, liberal arts

Other information:
Electronic University is, in effect, a clearinghouse which offers courses that can be taken from home using home computers. Students are linked directly over telephone lines to various universities, using software developed by Electronic University.

The list of participating schools changes frequently, but have included, for instance: Boston University, Ohio University, Penn State University, University of Illinois, and University of San Francisco.

While many schools offer courses through the Electronic University Network, at this time only three offer the opportunity to earn an external degree through EUN: a Bachelor's in many fields from Thomas Edison State College and from the University of the State of New York's Regents College (both described elsewhere in this book), and a Master's in business administration from Saginaw Valley State University.

Students must have an IBM, Apple II, or Commodore computer with telephone modem to connect with EUN's host computer. The student uses the computer to work on lessons and communicate with instructors, counselors, other students, and an electronic library. Professors are required to respond to questions left in the computer system by students within forty-eight hours.

Students have access to more than eighty computer data base systems, permitting them to tap into some large libraries while doing their coursework. The cost is from fourteen to sixty-five cents a minute.

Each course taken includes EUN course manual, textbooks, and software. Exams are taken locally, administered by local proctors. The network is available twenty-four hours a day.

Elizabethtown College

Accredited Bachelor's degrees in many fields, with a total of four days on campus.

Center for Continuing Education, EXCEL program
1 Alpha Drive
Elizabethtown, PA 17022

Telephone: (717) 367-1151
Fax number: —

Toll-free phone: —
Year established: 1899

Degree levels available: Bachelor's
Key person: Jim Voelker, EXCEL Program Coordinator
Recognition: Accredited by the Middle States Association
Ownership: Nonprofit, independent
Residency requirement: Four days

Tuition:
$2,160

Fields of study or special interest:
Accounting, business administration, communications, criminal justice, early childhood education, human services, medical technology, public administration

Other information:
Prospective students must have at least seven years work experience related to their major and fifty semester hours transfer credit from a regionally accredited institution. Applications are accepted only from people who live within a four-hundred-mile radius.

Students are required to attend four Saturday sessions on campus over a period of eighteen months.

Students may take courses from local colleges and apply the credit to their Elizabethtown degree. Credit also through Elizabethtown College courses, other approved courses (correspondence and residential), seminars, and approved special studies courses. Credit is also given for experiential learning.

Embry-Riddle Aeronautical University

Accredited nonresident degrees in aviation and business subjects, entirely through home study.

Department of Independent Studies
Daytona Beach, FL 32114

Telephone: (904) 239-6390 Toll-free phone: —
Fax number: (904) 239-6927 Year established: 1926

Degree levels available: Associate's, Bachelor's
Key person: Thomas W. Pettit, Director
Recognition: Accredited by the Southern Association
Ownership: Nonprofit, independent
Residency requirement: No residency required

Tuition:
$5,200 per year

Fields of study or special interest:
Professional aeronautics, aviation, business administration

Other information:
The degrees are available entirely through independent study courses. Each course includes a study guide, and a set of audio/videotapes. A textbook is also required for classes, but the cost is not included in fees. Twelve weeks are allowed to complete a course. A proctored final exam is required at the end of each course; some also have a midterm exam.

The program is designed for those with experience in civilian and military aviation only. To qualify, one must have certified civilian or military training and professional experience in any of the following specialties: air traffic control, airways facilities, airline command pilot, aviation safety, air carrier pilot, corporate pilot, flight technology, aircraft maintenance, aircraft dispatcher, commuter airline pilot, aviation weather, electronic operations and maintenance, flight operations administration, flight simulation, navigations systems, or certified flight instructor.

Up to thirty-six semester credit hours can be earned for previous aviation training and experience. Credit is also given for CLEP, USAFI, DANTES, E-RAU examinations, military service schools, aviation licenses and credentials, and transfer credit from accredited colleges.

# Empire State College

Accredited Associate's, Bachelor's, and Master's in many fields. Master's requires eight days on campus; the other degrees are nonresidential.

State University of New York
Saratoga Springs, NY 12866-4309

Telephone: (518) 587-2100
Fax number: —

Toll-free phone: —
Year established: 1971

Degree levels available: Associate's, Bachelor's, Master's
Key person: Walter Ulbricht, Director of College Relations
Recognition: Accredited by the Middle States Association
Ownership: Nonprofit, state
Residency requirement: No residency required

Tuition:
$45 per credit for New York residents *or* for those enrolled in the Center for Distance Learning. Full time tuition is about $2,100 a year.

Fields of study or special interest:
Associate's and Bachelor's in many fields in the liberal arts and sciences. Master's in business and policy studies, labor and policy studies, and culture and policy studies.

Other information:
The Bachelor's degree can be completed entirely at a distance. The Master of Arts requires four days on campus at the beginning and end of each semester.

Each student is assigned a mentor who helps plan and coordinate a course of study/individualized degree program within the college's eleven broad areas of undergraduate study.

The primary mode of instruction is independent study. The program is planned and organized through learning contracts, specific study plans for learning covering a particular period of time, including the study topic, means of study, amount of credit, and on what basis and by whom work will be evaluated.

The Center for Distance Learning offers structured courses and degree programs in interdisciplinary studies, human services, and business through correspondence courses. The student receives a study guide and text, and maintains contact with instructors by mail and phone.

Credit in all programs is given for relevant experiential learning. Empire State is a part of the State University of New York (not to be confused with the completely separate University of the State of New York), and has more than forty centers across New York state.

Eurotechnical Research University

Nonresident Doctorates in scientific fields, in the European research Doctorate model: No coursework, but extensive laboratory research.

P.O. Box 516
Hilo, HI 96721

Telephone: (808) 935-6424   Toll-free phone: —
Fax number: —   Year established: 1983

Degree levels available: Doctorates
Key person: James G. Holbrook, Ph.D., President
Recognition: Unaccredited; state registered
Ownership: Proprietary
Residency requirement: No residency required

Tuition:
$3,000 for complete program

Fields of study or special interest:
All scientific, technical, and engineering disciplines, including physics, chemistry, biology, nutrition, human health, and environmental studies.

Other information:
Eurotech's doctoral program is based on and follows exactly the pattern at the University of Southampton in England, with whom a formal link has been established.

In the tradition of the European research Doctorate, the degree is awarded solely on the basis of research plus the dissertation. Typically, the research is conducted in an industrial or government laboratory or other institution. The prospective enrollee seeks out a suitably qualified person in his or her organization to be the consulting professor, and proposes a research topic. If the university judges the qualifications of student and professor satisfactory, the project may proceed.

A mini-thesis must be submitted after the first year to demonstrate that work done so far is worth continuing. At this point the student is formally invited to stay at the school and become a candidate for the degree program. Minimum time for the entire degree program is two years. The quality of the final dissertation is judged by the consulting professor and an external examiner.

Eurotech's president prefers to discuss intended work, goals, and problems personally with each prospective student; thus inquirers are asked to provide a resumé or detailed letter with telephone number when inquiring. Applicants are evaluated on the criterion of their documented technical and professional merit. Most applicants will have a Master's degree and some research experience.

The university was established in California in 1983 and moved permanently to Hawaii in 1989.

Evergreen State College

The accredited Bachelor's and Master's require at least one meeting a month for at least nine months.

Olympia, WA 98505

Telephone: (206) 866-6000
Fax number: (206) 866-6823

Toll-free phone: —
Year established: 1967

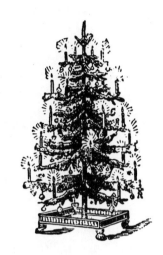

Degree levels available: Bachelor's, Master's
Key person: Christine Kerlin, Director of Admissions
Recognition: Accredited by the Northwest Association
Ownership: Nonprofit, state
Residency requirement: A meeting with faculty advisor once a month

Tuition:
$1,212 per year

Fields of study or special interest:
A great many fields

Other information:
Evergreen is primarily a residential school, albeit a nontraditional and highly innovative one, offering full-time interdisciplinary programs. However students have the option of creating "independent contract" courses of study for supervised research under a faculty mentor.

Groups of two or more students may work under a "group contract." Credit is given for internship programs, involving, for instance, work in local hospitals, clinics, or businesses. Students involved in independent study are still expected to visit the campus and meet with their faculty advisors at least once a month. All students must be enrolled for at least nine months before earning the degree.

While it is theoretically possible to live and work at a distance, the independent study program is more suitable for people living in the Pacific Northwest.

(My oldest daughter enjoyed Evergreen for the year she was there ["Go, Geoducks!"], but she came to prefer the more traditional programs at the University of California, Berkeley.)

Ferris State University

Accredited Bachelor's in industrial or environmental health by home study plus a three-week summer session on campus.

Gerholz Institute for Lifelong Learning
External Degree Program
Big Rapids, MI 49307

Telephone: (616) 592-2340   Toll-free phone: (800) 562-9130 (MI only)
Fax number: (616) 592-2990   Year established: 1884

Degree levels available: Bachelor's
Key person: Linda Broman
Recognition: Accredited by the North Central Association
Ownership: Nonprofit, state
Residency requirement: Three-week summer session on campus

Tuition:
$62 per credit hour for part-time students

Fields of study or special interest:
Industrial and environmental health management (for everyone); health systems management (available only in state of Michigan)

Other information:
Students may elect to satisfy requirements by means of courses which are offered by Ferris State on an external or correspondence study basis. The Bachelor of Science in environmental health is offered to people living anywhere in the United States through the School of Allied Health and the Gerholz Institute for Lifelong Learning. All of the course requirements for the degree can be met through an assessment of prior learning experience, or a combination of that plus equivalency examinations, independent study, faculty directed study, home study courses, and special projects.

Credit is given for experiential learning.

All students must attend a three-week summer session on campus. One year of work experience in the field of environmental health is required for admission to that program.

Fielding Institute

Accredited Master's and Doctorates in human and organization development, psychology and related areas, with a minimum of five days on campus.

2112 Santa Barbara Street
Santa Barbara, CA 93105

Telephone: (805) 687-1099
Fax number: —

Toll-free phone: —
Year established: 1974

Degree levels available: Master's, Doctorates
Key person: Donna Lucci, Director of Admissions
Recognition: Accredited by the Western Association
Ownership: Nonprofit, independent
Residency requirement: Five days minimum on campus

Tuition:
$6,360 per year

Fields of study or special interest:
Psychology (clinical and counseling), human and organization development, human services

Other information:
Five days are required on campus, but degrees are neither fast nor easy. The Master's takes at least two years; the various Doctorates from three to five years.

Before admission, one must have an interview with a faculty member. If accepted, applicants must attend a five-day Admissions Contract Workshop. It is here that the learning contract is developed. Workshops are held three times a year.

The work typically consists of guided independent study. Competency is demonstrated through research papers, exams, lectures, and professional reports.

The psychology degrees emphasize clinical or counseling and include a practicum and internship, research training, a doctoral dissertation, and an oral review. Although there are no rigid requirements about residency, there are times when a psychology student must appear on the campus.

Fielding does not accept transfer credit or give credit for prior experiential learning. Computer networking is used for communication between students and school. All students and faculty must have access to a computer with communication capability. Students in the same program meet regularly with Fielding faculty (cluster facilitators) for knowledge assessment, dissertation reviews, and seminars, as well as peer contact and support. There are thirty psychology and twelve HOD clusters located throughout the U.S.

Goddard College

Accredited Bachelor's and Master's in feminist studies, performing arts, and other fields, requiring several nine-day sessions on campus.

R.R. 2, Box 235
Plainfield, VT 05667

Telephone: (802) 454-8311   Toll-free phone: —
Fax number: —   Year established: 1938

Degree levels available: Bachelor's, Master's
Key person: Ellen Codling, Admissions Counselor
Recognition: Accredited by New England Association
Ownership: Nonprofit, independent
Residency requirement: Two nine-day sessions on campus or elsewhere

Tuition:
$2,613 for Bachelor's; $2,917 for Master's (both include room and board for the required nine-day meetings)

Fields of study or special interest:
Many fields, including business, history, visual and performing arts, multicultural studies, communications, literature, teacher education, and feminist studies

Other information:
The student comes to Goddard for nine days at the beginning of a semester for an All College meeting, to meet with a faculty advisor and plan the work to be done during the next semester.

Learning comes through doing (reading, writing, experimenting, creating, observing, etc.), and reflecting on doing (talking, keeping journals, etc.) Each student must write a letter-report to his or her faculty advisor every three weeks.

At the next nine-day meeting the student presents work done and is evaluated by self, advisor, and fellow students. Bachelor's and Master's require a minimum of one year enrollment at Goddard.

Students are expected to devote a minimum of twenty-six hours per week to study, and communicate with their advisor by mail every three weeks.

Goddard has worked with clusters of students at various locations around the U.S. and in Europe, where residential requirements could be met. The school has been a pioneer in nontraditional, progressive education for more than fifty years.

Grantham College of Engineering Technology

Accredited Bachelor's degree in engineering technology entirely by home study.

250 Frontage Road
P.O. Box 5700
Slidell, LA 70460

Telephone: (504) 646-1489
Fax number: —

Toll-free phone: (800) 955-2527
Year established: 1951

Degree levels available: Associate's, Bachelor's
Key person: Phillip Grantham, Administrative Vice President
Recognition: Accredited by the National Home Study Council
Ownership: Proprietary
Residency requirement: No residency required

Tuition:
$7,200 to $7,936 (depending on payment plan)

Fields of study or special interest:
Engineering technology, with emphasis in either computers or electronics

Other information:
The programs are designed for those who already have practical experience in the field and laboratory proficiency in electronics or computers (or will attain such proficiency before being awarded their degree). Grantham awards up to eighteen units of credit for work experience and lab proficiency.

Work is done through correspondence courses and independent home study. Each of four phases is designed to be completed in one year of part-time study. Students are given up to two years, but since it is self-paced, a highly motivated student may finish in less than one. Midphase and end of phase exams are given locally by proctors approved by the school. The entire program consists of 376 lessons and 4 examinations.

Students must transfer to Grantham with twenty-one units from another college (in English, history or social science, science, chemistry, and various electives). These units may have been earned by correspondence, equivalency exams or by taking classes. Each student must have access to a personal computer during some of the phases.

The Associate's degree is awarded "along the way" to the Bachelor's, after phase three.

Grantham's main rival, Cook Institute, makes a big point of the fact that Cook's degree is in electronics *engineering,* while Grantham's is in engineering *technology.*

In 1990, Grantham moved from California to Louisiana.

# Greenwich University

Nonresident Bachelor's, Master's, Doctorates, and Law degrees from the oldest school of its kind in the U.S.

100 Kamehameha Avenue
Hilo, HI 96720

Telephone: (808) 935-9934
Fax number: (808) 969-7469

Toll-free phone: (800) 367-4456 (U.S./Canada)
Year established: 1972

Degree levels available: Bachelor's, Master's, Doctorates, Law
Key person: John Bear, Ph.D., President
Recognition: Unaccredited; state registered
Ownership: Proprietary
Residency requirement: No Residency requirement

Tuition:

Ranges from $1,000 to $2,800 for complete degree programs, depending on amount of new work required

Fields of study or special interest:

Degrees can be earned in almost any field of study. There are structured or partly structured programs in business, health education, women's studies, computer science, Native American spirituality, and several others, but students are at work in everything from fisheries management to ethnomusicology to medical engineering.

Other information:

This is "my" school (I am full-time president), so of *course* I'm biased; I wouldn't be doing it if I didn't think it was good. The model is one of "filling in gaps." Student learning, however it occurred, is matched against our standards for what a degree-holder should know. Gaps are filled in through guided independent study, based on a learning contract developed by student and faculty mentors. A major paper, thesis or dissertation is required; it may be based on work done before enrolling.

The adjunct faculty of 150 includes many prominent scholars and authors. The two Deans of Students, resident in Hilo, are well-known educational authors and teachers, Drs. Rita and Stuart Johnson.

The Greenwich University School of Computer Sciences is based in Hong Kong, and offers a combined home-study and residential program. The School of Theology is based in England, and there is an office in Australia as well. But the main administrative center, where I sit, is our own ocean-front office building, the Greenwich University Building, in Hilo, Hawaii's second largest city.

The university is appropriately chartered by and registered with the state of Hawaii as a degree-granting institution. Degrees have been accepted by Fortune 500 companies, international organizations, and other universities.

Hawthorne University

Nonresident degree programs at all levels through home study.

155 East 3300 South
Salt Lake City, UT 84115

Telephone: (801) 485-1801
Fax number: (801) 485-1563

Toll-free phone: —
Year established: 1984

Degree levels available: Associate's, Bachelor's, Master's, Doctorates
Key person: Alfred W. Munzert, Ph.D., Chancellor
Recognition: Unaccredited; state registered
Ownership: —
Residency requirement: No Residency requirement

Tuition:
$895 per term for Utah residents; $3,000 per term out of state. Correspondence courses: $50 per semester hour. Video courses: $200 each.

Fields of study or special interest:
Degrees can be earned in almost any field of study.

Other information:
Hawthorne's Associate's degree is based on completion of twelve video courses, each involving twenty to thirty hours of viewing, oriented toward passing the CLEP exam in that area of study. The program is being expanded to include Bachelor's degrees.

The university has an arrangement with the Canadian School of Management, whereby people who complete the "Graduate" and "Fellow" degrees at CSM will be awarded the Bachelor's and Master's from Hawthorne.

Master's and Doctorates are offered through residential or independent study, under the supervision of university faculty.

Under the same management is an accredited high school, Hawthorne Academy, with a program in which students entering the eleventh grade typically complete two years of high school and two of college in two years.

Hawthorne's chancellor, Dr. Alfred W. Munzert, is the best-selling author of a variety of "test yourself" books, ranging from I.Q. to computer knowledge to ESP, and once authored a book on nontraditional higher education.

Henley, the Management College

Accredited British M.B.A. entirely through correspondence study.

Greenlands
Henley-on-Thames
Oxon, RG9 3AU England

Telephone: (0491) 571-454
Fax number: (0491) 571-635

Toll-free phone: —
Year established: 1946

Degree levels available: Master's
Key person: Jill Ford, Admissions Manager, Graduate Studies
Recognition: Equivalent of accreditation for England
Ownership: Nonprofit, independent
Residency requirement: No residency required

Tuition:
£4,700 (about $7,500)

Fields of study or special interest:
Business administration

Other information:
Henley offers its nonresident M.B.A. in association with Brunel University, which awards the degree.

Courses include texts, case studies, and audio and video cassettes. Exams are held either at Henley, at one of the Henley Network Centers worldwide, at a local educational establishment, or at a British Council Office.

Students write a dissertation (up to sixty pages), ideally dealing with a real problem for their own organization. There is tutorial support via computer. The computer may also be used to initiate conferences with fellow users and participate in conferences which are set up by experts in a particular field.

Workshops are offered for meeting tutors and fellow students prior to beginning the program and prior to exams. Workshops are considered to be desirable but not compulsory. They are given at Henley and other institutions affiliated with Henley Network Centers throughout the world (Australia, Cyprus, Denmark, Finland, Hong Kong, Malaysia, the Netherlands, Singapore, and three more in England).

The degree may be completed in a "standard" three-and-a-half-year program, or an accelerated two-year program. Applicants must have a Bachelor's degree and at least two years of organizational experience. A list of participants within the same area is available to all students. They are encouraged to form study and support groups.

Heriot-Watt University

Accredited Master's in construction management and in acoustics by videotape from Scotland.

Riccarton
Edinburgh, EH14 4AS Scotland

> Telephone: (031) 449-5111   Toll-free phone: —
> Fax number: —   Year established: 1966
>
> **Degree levels available:** Master's
> **Key person:** Dr. R. K. MacKenzie, Director of Studies
> **Recognition:** Equivalent of accredited, in Scotland
> **Ownership:** Nonprofit, independent
> **Residency requirement:** Short

Tuition:
£2,000 per year (about $3,200)

Fields of study or special interest:
Construction management, acoustics, vibration, and noise control

Other information:
The programs are designed for persons in building control and environmental health departments, or in inspection services. Students can live anywhere in the world. Acoustics, vibration, and noise control students must attend a one-week summer session, either in Scotland or in Hong Kong. Construction students must attend five one-week sessions during the course of the degree.

Courses are offered entirely by lecture on videotape. The video lectures, course notes, and tutorial exercises are based on the traditional program at the university. Both programs require courses plus a research project; construction management also requires a dissertation (in addition to the research project).

Exams are held once a year in Edinburgh, and at various overseas centers. Tutorial assistance is available from locally based tutors or by correspondence with staff at Edinburgh.

Honolulu University of Arts and Sciences and Humanities

Nonresident Bachelor's, Master's, and Doctorates in many fields of study.

1600 Kapiolani Boulevard
Honolulu, HI 96814

Telephone: (808) 955-7333   Toll-free phone: —
Fax number: —   Year established: 1978

Degree levels available: Bachelor's, Master's, Doctorates
Key person: Warren Walker, Ph.D., President
Recognition: Unaccredited, state registered
Ownership: —
Residency requirement: No residency required

Tuition:
$1,940 to $3,500

Fields of study or special interest:
Many fields

Other information:
Each student is assigned an advisor/mentor who helps him or her to develop a study plan for a particular degree, following the university's curriculum guidelines. The mentor is responsible for submitting a monthly progress report to the Academic Committee. Students keep in close contact with their advisors by phone, fax, and mail.

The university offers correspondence courses, with audio and video taped lectures. Credit is also given through mentor-guided reading programs and supervised independent study (projects, papers, etc.) or field study (conferences, internships, workshops, etc.) Courses may be challenged by taking an exam.

Most courses include a project or paper which is evaluated by the student's advisor. At the end of a course, the student submits a summary report covering course content, concepts learned, practicum experience, a bibliography substantiating depth and breadth of learning, and a self evaluation. The faculty advisor then assigns a number of credits and a letter grade.

No lower-division courses are offered. Bachelor's applicants must have completed those courses elsewhere or have equivalent life/work experience. All candidates for graduate degrees must complete a final project and submit a thesis or dissertation.

Former name: Golden State University, which operated from several cities in southern California.

Indiana Institute of Technology

Accredited Associate's and Bachelor's degrees in business and human services management through correspondence study.

1600 East Washington Boulevard
Fort Wayne, IN 46803

Telephone: (219) 422-5561   Toll-free phone: (800) 288-1766
Fax number: (219) 422-7696   Year established: 1930

Degree levels available: Associate's, Bachelor's
Key person: Don E. St. Clair, Director of Extended Study
Recognition: Accredited by North Central Association
Ownership: Nonprofit, independent
Residency requirement: No residency required

Tuition:
$140 per semester hour

Fields of study or special interest:
Business administration, human services management

Other information:
The degrees can be earned through independent study, primarily by use of correspondence courses, although some credit is given for life experience learning, and by examination.

The Institute also offers accelerated degree programs where, through intensive individual studies and weekly classroom sessions, one can complete a typical sixteen- to eighteen-week semester in as little as six weeks.

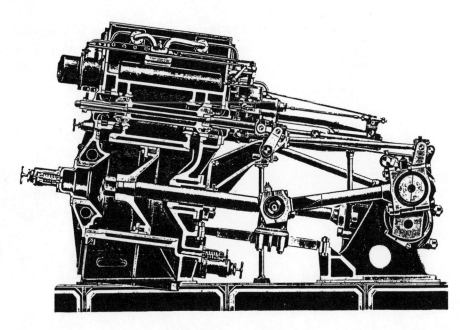

 # Indiana University

Accredited Associate and Bachelor of General Studies, without a major or in labor studies, entirely by correspondence study.

General Studies Degree Program
Division of Extended Studies
620 Union Drive, Room 543
Indianapolis, IN 46202

Telephone: (317) 274-3934   Toll-free phone: —
Fax number: —   Year established: 1975

Degree levels available: Associate's, Bachelor's
Key person: Louis Holtzclaw, Associate Director of Extended Studies for
    General Studies Degree
Recognition: Accredited by the North Central Association
Ownership: Nonprofit
Residency requirement: No residency required

Tuition:
$50 per credit hour

Fields of study or special interest:
General studies

Other information:
The Associate of General Studies and Bachelor of General Studies can be earned entirely through correspondence study. Students must complete fifteen and thirty units, respectively, after enrolling at the university.

The degree can be done without a major, or with a major in labor studies. One hundred twenty semester units are required. One quarter of the units must be upper division level. Credit is given for life experience learning, and a course is available in developing a portfolio.

Institute for the Advanced Study of Human Sexuality

Master's and Doctorates in various aspects of human sexuality, largely through home and independent study.

1523 Franklin Street
San Francisco, CA 94109

Telephone: (415) 928-1133   **Toll-free phone:** —
Fax number: —   **Year established:** 1976

Degree levels available: Master's, Doctorates
Key person: Robert T. McIlvenna, President
Recognition: Unaccredited, state approved
Ownership: Proprietary
Residency requirement: Very short

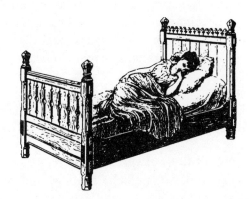

Tuition:
$2,300 per trimester

Fields of study or special interest:
Human sexuality, erotology, sex offender evaluation

Other information:
They believe there is a "woeful lack of professionals who are academically prepared in the study of human sexuality." The institute's intention is to rectify this lack by training professionals as sexologists.

Degrees offered include Master of Human Sexuality, Doctor of Human Sexuality (for therapists), Doctor of Education (for educators), and Doctor of Philosophy (stressing new knowledge and scientific inquiry). Also offers certificates in: sexological instructor of AIDS/STD prevention, erotology, and sex offender evaluation. Each Doctorate has a different emphasis: one in scientific enquiry, one in academic skills, and one in therapy and counseling.

There are three trimesters per year. A short time must be spent on campus for attending courses and lectures, but most work can be done at home. Many lectures are available on videotape. A comprehensive exam and a basic research project are required.

The Master's requires three trimesters of enrollment, and the Doctorate programs require five trimesters each.

Founders include prominent sexologists, such as Kinsey's coauthor, Wardell Pomeroy. Accreditation is claimed from the unrecognized but legitimate National Association for Private Non-traditional Schools and Colleges.

International Correspondence Institute

Accredited Associate's and Bachelor's degrees in religious subjects, entirely by correspondence study.

Chaussee de Waterloo, 45
1640 Rhode Saint Genese
Brussels, Belgium

Telephone: (02) 358-3510   Toll-free phone: —
Fax number: —   Year established: 1967

Degree levels available: Associate's, Bachelor's
Key person: George M. Flattery, Ed.D., President
Recognition: Accredited by the National Home Study Council
Ownership: Nonprofit, church
Residency requirement: No residency required

Tuition:
The literature states that "pricing information is available from the ICI national director in your area." I was not able to learn the costs.

Fields of study or special interest:
Bachelor of Arts in Bible/Theology, and Religious Education. Christian Ministry program is under development. Associate of Arts in religious studies.

Other information:
Their purpose is stated as "to win the lost, to develop the found, and to train workers for Christian ministry and service." The school began in Springfield, Missouri, and moved to Belgium in 1972. They have national offices in 110 countries.

The Institute produces its own self-study learning materials (which they call "teaching books") and also audio and video materials to be used with some courses. Some, but not all, courses include written assignments to be mailed in. Instructors are available for communication by mail and phone.

Final exams are sent sealed from the International Office to the national director who sends it to an exam supervisor who administers it to the student.

Some local seminars are arranged where selected subjects are taught in a classroom setting, often in conjunction with a local national ICI director or residential bible school. Credit may be received by taking only the final exam of a course. Fee is the same as taking the course. Credit is also given for experiential learning—up to one fourth of degree requirement, which totals thirty-two units. The fee for credit for experiential learning is the same as the academic charge for taking the course.

They have resident faculty whose main job is developing and teaching courses, and adjunct faculty who teach in field settings and serve as tutors to students studying independently.

International Correspondence Schools

Accredited Associate's in business by correspondence, and in technology with a one-week residency from America's pioneer correspondence school.

Center for Degree Studies
Scranton, PA 18515

Telephone: (717) 342-7701
Fax number: —

Toll-free phone: —
Year established: 1890

Degree levels available: Associate's
Key person: James S. Petorak, Director, Research and Testing
Recognition: Accredited by the National Home Study Council
Ownership: Proprietary
Residency requirement: No residency for one degree, one week for another

Tuition:
$2,751 to $3,366 (depending on degree)

Fields of study or special interest:
Associate in Specialized Business degree in business management or accounting
Associate in Specialized Technology degree in civil, electrical, and mechanical engineering and electronics technologies

Other information:
America's first significant correspondence school arose in Pennsylvania during the 1890s to provide education to coal miners. Now they provide it to untold thousands, through home study courses in business and technology.

Students are assigned work from courses produced by ICS. Instructors correct assignments, make criticisms, and can modify the program to meet the needs of each student.

Additional information is available through printed supplements to the courses, and a telecommunications network which links the student to the central office.

There are final exams at the end of each semester which may be taken locally, proctored by a proctor selected by ICS.

The business degree can be completed entirely by correspondence; the technology degree requires a residency of about one week.

International School of Information Management

Nonresident Master's in information management, which can be earned entirely by use of a home computer.

130 Cremona Drive
P.O. Box 1999
Santa Barbara, CA 93116

Telephone: (805) 685-1500
Fax number: —

Toll-free phone: (800) 441-4746
Year established: 1982

Degree levels available: Master's
Key person: Eric H. Boehm, Ph.D., President
Recognition: Unaccredited, state authorized
Ownership: Proprietary
Residency requirement: No residency required

Tuition:

1-unit course: $650; 2-unit course: $1,200 ; 3-unit course (most courses): $1,650; 4-unit course: $2,000. Course fees do not include ISIM on-line time fees. The school estimates that a Master's degree will cost between $27,000 and $30,000.

Fields of study or special interest:

Information resources management

Other information:

The instruction is delivered via a computer teleconferencing network. The program is available to students in the U.S. and Canada now; the rest of the world will come later.

Students need to be "teleliterate," and have a computer and telephone modem. The Institute offers a teleliteracy course on a tutorial basis.

For each course, the student receives a complete study guide, communications software, and study materials, such as textbooks and other written materials. Methods vary from instructor to instructor as to how competence is demonstrated, whether by projects, papers, written assignments, tests, etc.

Most coursework will be sent to the instructor by computer. Visual materials or materials not suitable for transmission via telecommunications may be sent by mail. Each course provides a public discussion area open to all course participants, who interact by computer conferencing. This area provides an open forum for discussions between students and faculty on topics relating to the course.

[SEE APPENDIX E REGARDING THE CHANGING SITUATION IN CALIFORNIA.]

Iowa State University

Accredited Bachelor of Liberal Studies available entirely by home study.

College of Sciences and Humanities
204 Carver Hall
Ames, IA 50011

Telephone: (515) 294-8300
Fax number: (515) 294-0565

Toll-free phone: (800) 262-3810
Year established: 1977

Degree levels available: Bachelor's
Key person: Kathleen Timmons
Recognition: Accredited by North Central Association
Ownership: Nonprofit, state
Residency requirement: No residency required

Tuition:
$1,825 per year

Fields of study or special interest:
Bachelor of Liberal Studies

Other information:
The Bachelor of Liberal Studies is primarily for residents of Iowa who are able to attend one of the off-campus centers around the state, or occasional courses on campus in Ames, although such residency is not mandatory. The program is designed specifically for those who have already earned sixty-two or more semester hours of college credit that may be applied to a liberal arts degree.

To complete the degree, students may earn credits through many study formats: television and telebridge courses ("telebridge" is a statewide system of two-way audio conferencing which permits classes to be held at remote locations), evening and weekend classes, on-campus classes, and correspondence classes. Students should check with an advisor to make sure any course they take will be acceptable to their degree program.

Of 124 units, 45 must come from a "four-year" college, 45 from an Iowa Regents University, and 30 from Iowa State University.

No traditional majors are available. Students choose to earn credits in three of five distribution areas (humanities, communications and arts, natural sciences and mathematical disciplines, social sciences, and professional fields).

 # Kansas State University

Accredited nonresident Bachelor's in interdisciplinary studies; a Master's is being planned.

Division of Continuing Education
College Court Building
Manhattan, KS 66506

Telephone: (913) 532-5687

Toll-free phone: (800) 432-8222 (KS)
(800) 255-2757 elsewhere

Fax number: (913) 532-5632

Year established: 1863

Degree levels available: Bachelor's (Master's to come)
Key person: Cynthia Trent, Non-Traditional Study Coordinator
Recognition: Accredited by the North Central Association
Ownership: Nonprofit, state
Residency requirement: No residency required

Tuition:
$55 per credit hour

Fields of study or special interest:
Interdisciplinary studies; possibly other fields

Other information:
At press time, the program was available only to Kansas residents, but the school reports "several exciting internal assessments and reviews of NTS operations have been made, and it appears that we will be operating with a larger program thrust."

In most cases students are required to have sixty units of college credit before applying to KSU nontraditional study. Students earn credit in a variety of ways: regular, on-campus courses including evening, summer, and short courses at KSU and other colleges in Kansas; community-based outreach courses, TELENET courses, television courses; independent study; correspondence coursework from other institutions, military training credit evaluations, guided studies, portfolio/experiential credit assessments, standardized test taking, credit by examination, competency assessments, and video and audio taped courses.

Degree requirements include a minimum of thirty KSU semester hours with twenty of the last thirty earned being from Kansas State. Total degree requirement is 120 units.

There are two new programs: "Second Wind" using the NTS program to reach out to former KSU athletes who left prior to graduation, and another, yet unnamed, which may lead to offering external Bachelor's and Master's degree programs, making use of an educational television network.

Kennedy-Western University

Nonresident Bachelor's, Master's, Doctorates, and Law degrees.

28310 Roadside Drive
Agoura Hills, CA 91301

Telephone: (818) 889-8443
Fax number: —

Toll-free phone: (800) 635-2900
Year established: 1984

Degree levels available: Bachelor's, Master's, Doctorates, Law
Key person: Paul Saltman, President
Recognition: Unaccredited, state authorized
Ownership: Proprietary
Residency requirement: No residency required

Tuition:
Bachelor's: $2,700 to $3,400; Master's $2,900 to $3,700; Doctorate: $3,200 to $4,150; Law: $3,500 to $4,200. $350 surcharge for students outside the U.S.

Fields of study or special interest:
Many fields, including business, health administration, criminal justice, education, and law.

Other information:
A formal interview is required before enrollment, in person or by telephone. Bachelor's applicants must have sixty semester units at college level or take a qualifying examination. All applicants must have five to seven years' experience in their field of study. Credit given for experiential learning, as well as prior college work and challenge exams.

New work is done through independent study. The student completes a study plan which sets forth goals, methods of meeting goals, time schedule, and criteria for evaluation of learning. The student's work will include such things as book critiques, case studies, and work-related research projects. All students must complete either a research project or a term paper/thesis/dissertation. Students who feel they have a "sophisticated level of expertise in their field and have already published" may petition for a final exam instead.

Law students may qualify to take the California bar exam. Academic work may be done in English or sixteen other languages.

I am concerned about the way Kennedy-Western misrepresents the findings of a 1978 government study on the acceptability of nontraditional degrees. The study was done with accredited Bachelor's degrees; the catalog implies it is relevant to unaccredited Doctorates as well.

[SEE APPENDIX E REGARDING THE CHANGING SITUATION IN CALIFORNIA.]

# Kensington University

Nonresident Bachelor's, Master's, Doctorates, and Law degrees.

124 South Isabel Street
P.O. Box 2036
Glendale, CA 91209

Telephone: (818) 240-9166
Fax number: (818) 240-1707

Toll-free phone: (800) 423-2495
Year established: 1976

Degree levels available: Bachelor's, Master's, Doctorates, Law
Key person: James H. Lambert, Ph.D., Ed.D., Director of Administration
Recognition: Unaccredited, state authorized
Ownership: Proprietary
Residency requirement: No residency required

Tuition:
$2,375 to $2,875 for entire program; law degrees $2,250 per year

Fields of study or special interest:
Law, business, behavioral and social sciences, engineering, education

Other information:
The programs are designed for the mature adult student who is capable of self-directed study. All coursework is accomplished by home study, with guidance and instruction provided by faculty advisors. Most coursework consists of guided, self-paced reading of assigned texts, and completion of a final project. Nonrequired seminars are offered periodically in Italy, Thailand, Japan, and England (where residential programs are available at the Bachelor's and Master's level through the facilities of City Commercial College in London). Law students qualify to take the bar exam, and they have had good success in recent years.

Kensington's bar preparation program (called Inns of Court) requires four years. Entering students must already have sixty semester units of college work. Each student is assigned a faculty advisor, who is a practicing attorney, to assist the student in all aspects of study. The advisor is available by phone or personal conference.

Nonbar programs (called Inns of Chancery) are for those who "do not wish to actively engage in the practice of law, but nevertheless wish to gain a better understanding of legal principles and procedures."

Like many other schools, Kensington misrepresents the findings of a government study on the acceptance of nontraditional degrees.

[SEE APPENDIX E REGARDING THE CHANGING SITUATION IN CALIFORNIA.]

La Jolla University

Bachelor's, Master's, and Doctorates largely through home study, with several short visits to La Jolla.

The La Jolla University Building
5005 Texas Street, 4th floor
San Diego, CA 92108

Telephone: (619) 293-3760
Fax number: —

Toll-free phone: —
Year established: 1977

Degree levels available: Bachelor's, Master's, Doctorates
Key person: Dr. Kamal L. Ranasinghe, President
Recognition: Unaccredited, state approved
Ownership: Proprietary
Residency requirement: Short residency

Tuition:
$100 to $120 per quarter unit

Fields of study or special interest:
Business and management, human behavior

Other information:
Working within the university's performance-based curriculum, learners participate in defining their emotional needs, goals, and aspirations, and then attend small evening/weekend classes and seminars. Some students are permitted to study on an independent basis, providing they keep pace with the resident programs. All students must come to San Diego for initial counseling, oral discussions, and defense of dissertations.

They also offer certificate programs in international relations, global policy studies, business studies, and protocol studies.

La Jolla admits students to its undergraduate degree programs if they have completed the equivalent of two years of university courses. Students may challenge courses by examination.

The university's former owner, Dr. Bernasconi, has registered a La Jolla University with Louisiana authorities, using a New Orleans address. At press time, I was attempting to discover the connection, if any, between the two La Jolla Universities.

The name, incidentally, is pronounced "La HOY-uh."

[SEE APPENDIX E REGARDING THE CHANGING SITUATION IN CALIFORNIA.]

# Lafayette University

Nonresident degrees at all levels through this school run by a branch of the Orthodox Catholic Church.

941 South Havana Street
Aurora, CO 80012

Telephone: (303)341-0082   Toll-free phone: —
Fax number: —   Year established: —

Degree levels available: Bachelor's, Master's, Doctorates
Key person: Thomas Wall, Director of Admissions
Recognition: Unaccredited (accredited by internal agency of the Church)
Ownership: Nonprofit, church
Residency requirement: Short residency

Tuition:
$120 to $140 per credit

Fields of study or special interest:
The catalog lists many, including liberal arts, business, some science (botany, conservation and wildlife, wellness sciences, nutritional sciences), metaphysics, psychotherapy, religion (divinity studies, religious education, pastoral wellness, theology, pastoral psychotherapy)

Other information:
The university is affiliated with the Mercian Rite (Orthodox) Catholic Church. Students are allowed to assist in designing their own academic programs (they design their own graduate degree study programs within parameters set by the university). Degrees through correspondence require one to two weeks attendance at the school.

The 1989 catalog states that Lafayette is "the only accredited institution in the U.S." offering degree courses in nutrimedical arts and sciences. No nutrimedical courses are listed. Lafayette's accreditation comes from the church's own Department of Education and Academic Affairs which "has the authority within our own church to charter and accredit . . ."

Former Vice President Father Thompson writes "Please know that Lafayette University is state accredited." However, the Colorado Commission on Higher Education does not accredit schools, and has written that Lafayette "marginally qualifies" for state *authorization.*

The program seems academically sound, but some of the claims made are a cause for concern.

 # Liberty University

Accredited Associate's, Bachelor's, and Master's in business and religious fields with as little as one week on campus, perhaps less.

School of Life Long Learning
Box 11803
Lynchburg, VA 24506

Telephone: (804) 522-4700
Fax number: —

Toll-free phone: (800) 446-5000
Year established: 1971

Degree levels available: Associate's, Bachelor's, Master's
Key person: Thomas Diggs, Dean, School of Life Long Learning
Recognition: Accredited by the Southern Association
Ownership: Nonprofit, church
Residency requirement: One week or less on campus

Tuition:
$115 per semester hour

Fields of study or special interest:
Associate of Arts in religion, Bachelor's in church ministries, business, and business management, Master's in Biblical studies, counseling and business administration.

Other information:
Prospective students are assessed according to academic background, moral character, and personal testimony for Jesus. Residential students must have accepted Jesus as their personal savior; nonresidential are not required to have done so.

There is no limit to credit for transferring units or for experiential learning. Challenge exams are given for each course.

While several courses are normally required to be completed on campus for each degree, "Students with unique cases, such as military personnel and senior citizens will have their requirements for residency evaluated," and may need to spend as little as a week, perhaps less, on campus. When required, residential courses are offered through one- or two-week intensive courses during summer and selected holidays.

All courses are provided on VHS videotapes. Students receive a textbook and workbook as well as the video. Exams are given locally by proctors. Faculty are regularly available by telephone. Liberty's chancellor is Dr. Jerry Falwell.

More than a few readers have complained to me about the "hard sell" recruiting that goes on once one has inquired here, but the complaints have all related to the marketing of the school, not the school itself.

Mary Baldwin College

Accredited Bachelor's degree in many fields, entirely by home study, except for two days on campus in Virginia.

Adult Degree Program
Staunton, VA 24401

> Telephone: (703) 887-7000   Toll-free phone: —
> Fax number: —   Year established: 1842
>
> **Degree levels available:** Bachelor's
> **Key person:** James Harrington, Director
> **Recognition:** Accredited by the Southern Association
> **Ownership:** Nonprofit, independent
> **Residency requirement:** Two days on campus

Tuition:
$2,600 annually plus $95 per semester hour (classes and independent study)

Fields of study or special interest:
Many fields (independent majors may also be designed)

Other information:
All students attend a two-day orientation on campus. Each student works with an advisor to design a program.

Credit is available through courses at Mary Baldwin or other accredited institutions, independent study (tutorials) under the supervision of Mary Baldwin faculty or approved off-campus tutors, and accredited, approved correspondence courses. Credit is also given for experiential learning, transfer credit from other schools, and equivalency examinations.

The Bachelor's degree requires 132 semester credit hours, incorporating a "balance of breadth in the liberal arts" and depth in a major area of study.

The degree requires a minimum of nine months to complete. The degree program has regional offices in several other Virginia cities.

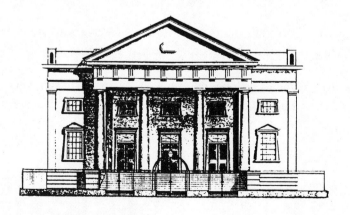

Marywood College

Accredited Bachelor's degrees in accounting or business administration by correspondence plus a two-week session on campus.

2300 Adams Avenue
Scranton, PA 18509

Telephone: (717) 348-6235
Fax number: (717) 348-1817

Toll-free phone: —
Year established: 1915

Degree levels available: Bachelor's
Key person: Registrar
Recognition: Accredited by the Middle States Association
Ownership: Nonprofit
Residency requirement: Two weeks on campus

Tuition:
$135 per semester credit, which includes cost of textbooks

Fields of study or special interest:
Bachelor of Science in accounting or business administration

Other information:
Students who wish to apply to the off-campus program must be at least eighteen years old and live more than fifty miles from Marywood. One hundred twenty-six semester hours are required for a degree. Sixty must be earned after enrolling at Marywood. Credit is given for experiential learning (nearly half the required credit can come from this as well as equivalency exams).

Courses are conducted by guided independent study. The student is sent "instruction units" consisting of texts, study guide, and assignments. Communication with teachers is by mail and phone. Courses require proctored exams.Credit can also be earned by completing independent study projects.

A student who has substantial transfer credit will have to spend one two-week session on campus. Other students must spend two two-week periods on campus, one midway through the program, and one at the end.

The Off-Campus Degree Program offers a free "Dial-a-Question" service.

Deferred payment plans are available.

Mind Extension University

An accredited M.B.A. from Colorado State University can be earned entirely through courses offered by cable television.

9697 East Mineral Avenue
Englewood, CO 80112-9920

Telephone: —

Fax number: —

Toll-free phone: (800) 777-6463

Year established: —

Degree levels available: Master's
Key person: Registrar
Recognition: Accredited degree available
Ownership: —
Residency requirement: No residency required

Tuition:
$300 per semester credit thus $18,900 for M.B.A. plus $1,000 for books

Fields of study or special interest:
Many fields of study offered; degree is in business administration

Other information:
Instruction is by telecourses. Mind Extension University televises courses twenty-four hours a day over the university's own cable channel, nationwide. The individual courses are produced by different universities.

Class materials and coursework are sent by mail. MEU provides a toll-free number to facilitate phone communication between student and instructor. Exams are given by proctor.

A student enrolls in MEU and receives credit from an MEU affiliated school (there are twelve).

At this time, the only complete degree program which can be completed with telecourses is an accredited M.B.A. program from Colorado State University. The M.B.A. requires sixty-three semester units although some may be waived if the equivalent has been done elsewhere.

For people who do not have access to the MEU channel, it may be possible to buy or rent the videotapes directly from Colorado State University.

Students work by mail and phone with an instructor from the college offering the course.

I have spent a fair amount of time watching MEU on my local cable channel. The courses are prepared by each individual instructor and, just like any on-campus education, range from lively and engaging to dry and tedious.

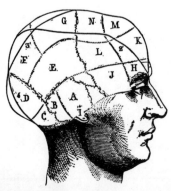

National Technological University

Accredited Master's in engineering, computer science, management and related areas, by viewing televised courses locally.

700 Centre Avenue
Fort Collins, CO 80526

Telephone: (303) 484-6050   Toll-free phone: —
Fax number: (303) 484-0668   Year established: 1984

Degree levels available: Master's
Key person: Lionel Baldwin
Recognition: Accredited by the North Central Association
Ownership: Nonprofit, independent
Residency requirement: View courses locally by television

Tuition:
$425 per credit and up

Fields of study or special interest:
Computer engineering, computer science, electrical engineering, management, manufacturing systems engineering, materials science, and management of technology

Other information:
The university has developed a wide range of courses in technological subjects. These are transmitted by satellite television to more than thirty campuses, from Alaska to Florida, to participating businesses, where students take the classes, often in "real time" (as they are being taken at various universities), with telephone links to the Colorado classroom. NTU offers its own Master of Science degree, available in the same model, in computer engineering, computer science, electrical engineering, engineering management, manufacturing systems engineering, materials science, and management of technology.

 # Newport University

Nonresident degrees at all levels, including Law, entirely through home study.

3720 Campus Drive
Newport Beach, CA 92660

Telephone: (714) 756-8297   Toll-free phone: —
Fax number: —   Year established: 1976

Degree levels available: Associate's, Bachelor's, Master's, Doctorates, Law
Key person: Dr. Ted Dalton, President
Recognition: Unaccredited, state approved
Ownership: Proprietary
Residency requirement: No residency required

Tuition:
$70 per unit

Fields of study or special interest:
Business administration, law, education, engineering, psychology, human behavior, religion, general studies (Associate's only)

Other information:
They offer an "Individualized Education Program" based on "Directed Independent Study." For every course the student will be sent a syllabus which will identify each concept or idea considered to be of importance to that course and will advise which text to use. It will also include "performance requirements"—how to prove to the student's faculty advisor that he or she understands the concepts of the course.

Each student is assigned a faculty member (educational facilitator) for each course with whom they keep in touch by mail and phone.

A senior paper is required for the Bachelor's. A thesis is strongly recommended for the Master's, but may be waived and replaced by two courses. A dissertation is recommended for the Doctorate, but it may be replaced by three courses with approval of the Dean.

Credit is given for experiential learning at the undergraduate level only.

Newport has representatives or branch offices in fifteen countries.

Original name: Newport International University.

Students of the four-year bar preparation program qualify to take the California bar exam.

[SEE APPENDIX E REGARDING THE CHANGING SITUATION IN CALIFORNIA.]

Northwood Institute

Accredited Associate's and Bachelor of Business Administration with a total of seven days required on campus.

3225 Cook Road
Midland, MI 48640

Telephone: (517) 832-4411   Toll-free phone: —
Fax number: (517) 832-9590   Year established: 1959

Degree levels available: Associate's, Bachelor's
Key person: Robert Serum, Ph.D., Dean, External Plan of Study
Recognition: Accredited by the North Central Association
Ownership: Nonprofit, independent
Residency requirement: Seven days on campus

Tuition:
Correspondence coursework and weekend classes, $35 per credit hour; $420 fee for experiential credit evaluation, $560 fee for Final Comprehensive Exam.

Fields of study or special interest:
Associate of Arts in twelve fields (including accounting, advertising, banking/finance, fashion marketing and merchandising, fire science management); Bachelor of Business Administration with eight different majors (management is the most popular)

Other information:
All Bachelor of Business Administration students are required to attend two three-day seminars on campus (focusing on "updating business management"). Certain programs may require more on-campus coursework (for example some computer classes that have labs). All BBA students are required to complete a thesis project and to take a comprehensive oral and written exam on campus as the last step in their program. The exam will last for several hours and will be based on questions provided to the students in advance.

Credit is given for experiential learning, equivalency exams, and transfer credit (up to 144 credits). Degree coursework can be completed in the following ways:

◆ Weekend college classes. Special classes are arranged at various times and places.
◆ Open-book Comprehensive Examinations. Students research answers to highly structured topics, questions, and exercises. Suggested references are provided. Student submits completed material for evaluation by a professor.
◆ Project Courses. Selected courses are available on a project basis. Project courses often relate to a student's employment and tie in with specific work-related areas that have correlation to the course of study. Students write a twenty-five to thirty page report on their projects.
◆ Correspondence Courses. Courses consisting of a series of lessons evaluated by a professor on a lesson-by-lesson basis. All courses require a proctored exam. These courses have a ninety-day time limit.
◆ Approved college courses at other colleges.
◆ Northwood offers its external degree programs through offices or centers in ten other states.

 # Nova University

Accredited Bachelor's, Master's, and Doctorates largely through independent study, with occasional group meetings and seminars at various locations.

3301 College Avenue
Fort Lauderdale, FL 33314

Telephone: (305) 475-7413   Toll-free phone: —
Fax number: (305) 476-1999   Year established: 1964

Degree levels available: Bachelor's, Master's, Doctorate
Key person: Abraham Fischler, President
Recognition: Accredited by the Southern Association
Ownership: Nonprofit, independent
Residency requirement: Varies; typically 30 to 40 days, spread out over several years

Tuition:
Varies according to the program and circumstances, but a Doctorate will cost in excess of $20,000.

Fields of study or special interest:
Educational administration, teacher education, business administration, including international management, public administration, computer studies, and information science.

Other information:
Nova University has one of the more nontraditional Master's and Doctorate programs ever to achieve regional accreditation. Residential seminars and "institutes" have been held in as many as twenty-three states, and Nova will consider offering the program wherever a cluster of twenty to twenty-five students can be formed in the continental U.S.

One- or two-week-long "Institutes" at NU are required, as well as group meetings (may be one a month), and from three to six practicums which emphasize direct application of research to the work place.

Some programs are offered by the Center for Computer Based Learning. For these programs students need to have a computer and modem for on-line electronic communication. The student uses the computer for instruction, tutoring, and conferences with other students. A major part of instruction in this program is through teleconferencing, TELNET, and TYME. These CBL programs also utilize regional and on-campus seminars. Doctoral programs are offered in information science (for librarians and information managers), training and learning (deals with development and implementation of training programs), information systems, and education.

"Field based" Bachelor's, Master's, and Doctorates are offered in computer science, education, higher education, and educational leadership. These programs require that the student be employed in the field of study. Instruction is through directed study and applied research.

 # Ohio University

Accredited Associate's and a very inexpensive Bachelor of General Studies entirely through home study.

Adult Learning Services, External Student Program
301 Tupper Hall
Athens, OH 45701

Telephone: (614) 593-2150   Toll-free phone: (800) 444-2420
Fax number: (614) 593-4229   Year established: 1804

Degree levels available: Associate's, Bachelor's
Key person: Michael Mark, Director of Adult Learning Services
Recognition: Accredited by the North Central Association
Ownership: Nonprofit, state
Residency requirement: No residency required

Tuition:
$39 per quarter hour for independent study courses; $21 per quarter hour course for credit by examination.

Fields of study or special interest:
Associate's in Arts, Science, and Individualized Studies; Bachelor of General Studies

Other information:
The Bachelor of General Studies offers an opportunity to design an individualized four-year degree plan, working with an advisor on the degree proposal. The degree requires 192 "quarter" hours (equivalent to 128 semester hours), including an area of concentration of 45 hours.

Credit is given for experiential learning. To earn it, a student must enroll in a four-hour, graded, independent study course. A student may earn up to one quarter of the degree credits through experiential learning. Other credit is earned through independent study and correspondence courses. Student receives study guide, texts, etc. Each course requires lessons to be submitted, as well as a paper/project and generally a midterm, and a final exam.

Credit may also be received by enrolling in Course Credit by Examination. The student enrolls in a course and receives only a brief syllabus describing the nature of the course, texts, and materials to study. The student prepares for the exam on his or her own, without teachers' assistance. When he or she is ready, the student takes the exam. These exams can be administered anywhere in the world and must be supervised.

Independent study projects are also a possibility if a course the student wants is not available by correspondence. The External Student Program provides a counseling and advising service, and also acts as a liaison in dealing with other university offices.

A total of forty-eight quarter hours must be earned at Ohio University after enrollment. If the work is done by correspondence course, the total cost for the Bachelor's could be under $1,000.

Oklahoma City University

Accredited Bachelor's degree through independent study, with a minimum time of sixteen weeks, and one short visit to the campus.

Competency Based Degree Program
2501 North Blackwelder
Oklahoma City, OK 73106

Telephone: (405) 521-5265   Toll-free phone: —
Fax number: (405) 521-5264   Year established: 1901

Degree levels available: Bachelor's
Key person: Denise Short, Director
Recognition: Accredited by the North Central Association
Ownership: Nonprofit
Residency requirement: Short

Tuition:
$4,558 per year

Fields of study or special interest:
Many fields

Other information:
A Bachelor of Arts or Science degree can be earned by granting university course credit for knowledge you already have and helping you attain credits you need without spending hours in the classroom. Possible alternatives to traditional study may be available.

Students must be at least twenty-five years of age, and be able to visit the campus for an Orientation Workshop. Because the program involves a great deal of student/faculty interaction, more than one visit may be necessary. All students must be enrolled for at least sixteen weeks before earning the degree. This program is not intended to be a correspondence program.

Credit can be earned through traditional classroom work, independent study, directed readings, experiential learning, or a combination of these methods.

Each student works with a coordinator to determine the areas of study in which the student needs to gain competence, and also how best to fulfill the degree requirements.

Open Learning for the Fire Service Program

Accredited Bachelor's degree in fire service areas, through correspondence courses taken from any of seven universities and colleges.

National Fire Academy
16825 South Seton Avenue
Emmitsburg, MD 21727

Telephone: (301) 447-1127
Fax number: —

Toll-free phone: —
Year established: 1977

Degree levels available: Bachelor's
Key person: Edward J. Kaplan, MSPA, Project Officer
Recognition: Accredited courses
Ownership: Nonprofit
Residency requirement: No residency required

Tuition:
Varies with each school

Fields of study or special interest:
Fire administration, fire prevention technology

Other information:
The program is offered through seven regional colleges (all accredited): Cogswell College (California), University of Cincinnati, Memphis State University, Western Oregon State College, The University of Maryland University College, Western Illinois University, and Empire State College.

All work is done by correspondence study. Students are sent a course guide, required textbooks, and their assignments. They communicate with instructors by mail and telephone. Supervised exams can be taken locally.

Western Illinois and Empire State offer degrees nonresidentially. At the other schools, one earns credit toward the degree, but would have to do other work at the school.

 # Open University

Accredited nonresident degrees at all levels, through home study, ostensibly for U.K. residents only.

Walton Hall
Milton Keynes, MK7 6AA England

Telephone: (0908) 274066   Toll-free phone: —
Fax number: —   Year established: 1969

Degree levels available: Bachelor's, Master's, Doctorates
Key person: Ralph Keats, Assistant Registrar
Recognition: Equivalent of accredited in England
Ownership: Nonprofit
Residency requirement: No residency required

Tuition:

£188 per credit; £103 for a week-long seminar (roughly equivalent to $320 per credit; $175 for the seminar)

Fields of study or special interest:

Social sciences, science and technology, education, literature, and mathematics

Other information:

England's highly innovative and largest nontraditional university has become the model for similar ventures worldwide. Degrees at all levels are offered through a combination of home study texts, radio and television programs, audio and video cassettes, week-long seminars during the summer months, and home laboratory kits for science students. A Bachelor's degree can take anywhere from three to six years of part-time study; a Doctorate from three to nine years.

About thirty hours of broadcast material are transmitted each week on BBC radio and television. The Open University is increasing its use of cassette material. There are currently more than seventy thousand undergraduate students and well over one thousand graduate students registered.

Open University was started as an experiment in 1971, and has grown into the most elaborate correspondence school in the world. As at other British universities, credit is earned only by passing examinations.

Open University did not wish to be included in this book, and would not cooperate by supplying information. Perhaps they are annoyed with me for reporting, in an earlier edition, that more than a few students outside England are enrolled, using a convenience address in Britain. That is strictly forbidden, and not encouraged, but all I did was report the facts.

Oral Roberts University

Accredited Bachelor's degree in religious subjects or elementary education by home study with one week per semester on campus.

Center for Lifelong Education
7777 South Lewis Avenue
Tulsa, OK 74171

Telephone: (918) 495-6161
Fax number: (918) 495-6478

Toll-free phone: (800) 678-8876
Year established: 1965

Degree levels available: Bachelor's
Key person: Frances Yager, Co-ordinator
Recognition: Accredited by the North Central Association
Ownership: Nonprofit, church
Residency requirement: One week per semester

Tuition:
$85 per semester hour

Fields of study or special interest:
Christian care and counseling, elementary education, church ministries

Other information:
Instruction is by correspondence study, with credit given for experiential learning and equivalency exams. Local mentors, in various locations, work with students in a learning contract model. Many of the courses are on audio cassettes, and computers are used.

One week per semester is required on campus.

Applicants must sign a pledge not to use tobacco or alcohol, not to lie, cheat, curse, or steal, to participate in an aerobics program, attend church, avoid homosexual behavior, and commit their lives to Jesus.

In literature sent in response to an inquiry, forty of the forty-three pages related to financial aid.

 # Ottawa University

Accredited Bachelor's and Master's degrees primarily through home study, with a few short visits to the campus or centers in other locations.

10th and Cedar
Ottawa, KS 66067

Telephone: (913) 242-5200   Toll-free phone: (800) 255-6380
Fax number: (913) 242-7429   Year established: 1865

Degree levels available: Bachelor's, Master's
Key person: Richard Maack, Director of Admissions
Recognition: Accredited by North Central Association
Ownership: Nonprofit
Residency requirement: Short

Tuition:
$115 per semester hour for undergraduate; $165 per credit hour for graduate

Fields of study or special interest:
Many fields for Bachelor's degree; Master's in human resources.

Other information:
Each student needs to take an initial "proseminar" which "engages the student in learning and skill development." Then the student builds a degree plan (another required course). A final required course is a graduate review at the end of studies. Only a few short visits to the campus are required; all work in between is done through guided independent study. Each student has a faculty advisor who helps plan the program, and works with them throughout.

In the Bachelor's degree plan, the student must demonstrate competence in four breadth areas: communication, social/civic, lifelong learning, and values, and complete a "major"—an in-depth area of study consisting of at least twenty-eight semester hours of coursework.

Degree requirements are met through traditional scheduled courses, and directed study (individualized independent study), "a course that by its design assumes an enrolled student is able to master the material through individualized instruction."

Classes are offered year round in eight-week sessions. One can begin a program at any time during the year.

The university has adult centers in Kansas City and Phoenix, and offices in Hong Kong, Taiwan, Singapore, and Malaysia. Administratively, OU is one university located in three domestic sites. It also operates in Hong Kong, Taiwan, Singapore, and Malaysia.

Pacific Southern University

Nonresident Bachelor's, Master's and Doctorates in several fields through home study.

9581 West Pico Boulevard
Los Angeles, CA 90035

Telephone: (213) 551-0304   Toll-free phone: —
Fax number: —   Year established: 1978

Degree levels available: Bachelor's, Master's, Doctorates
Key person: Javad Khazrai, Ph.D., President
Recognition: Unaccredited, state authorized
Ownership: Proprietary
Residency requirement: No residency required

Tuition:
$2,950 to $3,750 for complete program.

Fields of study or special interest:
Business administration (all levels) and engineering (Bachelor's and Master's only)

Other information:
Degrees in other subjects may be available "in special circumstances." Credit is given for experiential learning.

The student studying through independent study is provided with materials (texts, audio and videotapes, and tests). A faculty advisor will be assigned who will coordinate study assignments and completion dates (mutually agreed upon by advisor and student). The advisor will also establish testing dates and monitor the progress of the student.

Bachelor's students may obtain up to ninety units through comprehensive equivalency exams given to the student by a proctor locally. They are also required to write an undergraduate thesis.

Master's students must complete a thesis, and Ph.D. students must complete dissertation and sit for an oral examination.

[SEE APPENDIX E REGARDING THE CHANGING SITUATION IN CALIFORNIA.]

 **Pacific Western University**

Nonresident Bachelor's, Master's, and Doctorates entirely through home study.

7 Waterfront Plaza
500 Ala Moana Boulevard
Honolulu, HI 96813

Telephone: (808) 526-3966
Fax number: —

Toll-free phone: (800) 423-3244
Year established: 1977

Degree levels available: Bachelor's, Master's, Doctorates
Key person: Philip Forte, President
Recognition: Unaccredited, registered with state
Ownership: Proprietary
Residency requirement: No residency required

Tuition:
$2,095 to $2,395 for complete program

Fields of study or special interest:
Business, management science, engineering, physical and natural science, social science, education, and the helping professions

Other information:
The literature reports that "all degree programs are primarily based on what the student has already learned. . . . If the student is worthy, competent, and eminently qualified, the University will confer the appropriate degree."

The program includes preparation of a resumé/learning portfolio, a degree program "warrant" (a six-hundred-word essay concerning student's career field), a Bachelor's thesis (eight pages) or qualifying exercise (twelve pages), or a Master's project or Doctoral dissertation.

If students lack credits, special study programs or projects may be devised and assigned. The school says they are "most effective with persons who have virtually earned their degrees, although those degrees were not formally recognized."

In 1989, Pacific Western began offering Doctorates through its office in Hawaii while continuing to offer Bachelor's and Master's through its California offices. In 1990, the school was using addresses in Hawaii and Louisiana, while continuing to occupy its own handsome building in California, apparently waiting to see which way the winds were blowing in California.

[SEE APPENDIX E REGARDING THE CHANGING SITUATION IN CALIFORNIA.]

Prescott College

Accredited Bachelor's in management, psychology, and other areas by home study, with two weekends on campus in Arizona.

Adult Degree Program
220 Grove Avenue
Prescott, AZ 86301

Telephone: (602) 778-2090
Fax number: (602) 776-0724

Toll-free phone: —
Year established: 1966

Degree levels available: Bachelor's
Key person: Jan Buford, Admissions Co-ordinator, Adult Degree Program
Recognition: Accredited by the North Central Association
Ownership: Nonprofit, independent
Residency requirement: Two weekends on campus

Tuition:
$2,250, full time (18–23 credit hours) per six-month period, or $105 per credit hour

Fields of study or special interest:
Management, business administration, human services, counseling, psychology, teacher education, plus individually designed liberal arts majors

Other information:
All students are required to attend a weekend orientation at the beginning of their program and one weekend seminar during enrollment. Students normally take two courses every three months.

Each student develops the structure of her or his degree program with an advisor. Students also work with various mentors to determine the structure and content of individual independent study "courses." A learning contract is written by the student with the mentor at the beginning of each course, and must be approved by the ADP office.

With the help of Prescott's staff, students develop a network of adjunct faculty in their own community, who serve as independent-study mentors. Students meet weekly with those mentors.

Every program includes an internship or experiential component (related to job, student teaching, or research project) in the student's field.

Graduation is not based on number of units earned, but on demonstration of competence. Students write a graduation proposal demonstrating and documenting their learning.

Entering students normally have a minimum of thirty semester hours of college work. One year of enrollment at Prescott is required to earn a degree. Credit is given for life experience through writing a life experience portfolio.

 # Regis College

Accredited Bachelor's in a University Without Walls program requiring only one orientation session on campus.

West 50th Avenue and Lowell Boulevard
Denver, CO 80221

Telephone: (303) 458-4300
Fax number: (303) 458-4129

Toll-free phone: (800) 727-6399
Year established: 1877

Degree levels available: Bachelor's
Key person: Director of Admissions
Recognition: Accredited by North Central Association
Ownership: Nonprofit, church
Residency requirement: Very short

Tuition:
$8,600 per year

Fields of study or special interest:
Student chooses own field, or selects from among business administration, computer information systems, and management. (They also offer teachers certification for early childhood, elementary, middle school, and secondary education.)

Other information:
Regis operates a University Without Walls program, in which students develop their own program in consultation with a faculty advisor. The degree program may include regular college classes (at Regis or any other accredited school), internships, company-sponsored training, and independent study.

In the independent study mode, for each subject of interest, the student selects a course consultant (someone who holds at least a Master's degree in the subject) and together with that consultant and their faculty advisor, writes a learning contract (what will be learned, how, and how it will be evaluated).

Credit is also earned for work/life experience (including military training), and courses can be challenged (by exam).

Students must attend one orientation session prior to registration.

Roger Williams College

Accredited Associate's and Bachelor's in engineering, writing, technology, and many other fields, largely through nonresident study.

The Open Program
School of Continuing Education
Bristol, RI 02809

Telephone: (401) 253-1990
Fax number: (401) 254-0490

Toll-free phone: —
Year established: 1974

Degree levels available: Associate's, Bachelor's
Key person: Robert Fettrerhoff, Registrar
Recognition: Accredited by the New England Association
Ownership: Nonprofit, independent
Residency requirement: No residency required

Tuition:
$8,835 per year

Fields of study or special interest:
Many fields including engineering and industrial technology, career writing, historic preservation, marine biology, and theater

Other information:
Up to 75 percent of necessary units for the degrees can be earned through an assessment of prior learning, equivalency exams, etc. The assessment is based on a portfolio, oral interviews, and tests. Assessment takes two to five months, and there is no extra charge for it.

Students may enter as "long distance students" only if they enter with advanced academic standing and sufficient educational resources available to them locally.

Although there are no specific on-campus requirements, most students will visit the campus to meet with their faculty advisor, and to prepare academic records, for formulation of program design, review of credit documentation, and preliminary meetings with adjunct faculty.

Instructional methods used include classroom courses (day, evening, and summer), external courses, internships, independent study, correspondence courses, and courses from other colleges.

Besides Associate's and Bachelor's degrees, they also offer certificate programs in surveying, paralegal studies, school nurse teaching, chemical dependency, human resource development, and construction science.

Saint Edwards University

Accredited Bachelor of Liberal Studies, mostly available by home study, but with one class on campus.

New College
3001 South Congress
Austin, TX 78704

Telephone: (512) 448-8717
Fax number: (512) 448-8492

Toll-free phone: —
Year established: 1885

Degree levels available: Bachelor's
Key person: Carol Hussey, Registrar
Recognition: Accredited by the Southern Association
Ownership: Nonprofit, independent
Residency requirement: Some

Tuition:
$236 per credit hour (one third of that for challenge exams)

Fields of study or special interest:
Bachelor of Liberal Studies in many fields, including business, humanities, and social sciences

Other information:
Thirty units must be earned after admission, but all but three of these can come from off-campus or independent study, assessment of prior learning, and equivalency exams. Credit is given for experiential learning. The assessment is based on analysis of a portfolio prepared by the student in a special research course offered for that purpose. The cost is based on a fee for each credit awarded.

With an advisor, the student designs a degree plan in conformity with the New College curriculum design.

Saint Joseph's College

Accredited Bachelor's and Master's requiring two to three weeks on campus, including a Professional Arts degree for registered nurses only.

External Degree Program
Department 840
Windham, ME 04062

Telephone: (207) 892-7841
Fax number: (207) 892-7480

Toll-free phone: (800) 552-2201 (ME only)
Year established: 1912

Degree levels available: Bachelor's, Master's
Key person: Patricia Sparks, Dean, External Degree Program
Recognition: Accredited by the New England Association
Ownership: Nonprofit, church
Residency requirement: Two or three weeks

Tuition:
$150 per credit (minimum of 2 courses, 3 credits each)

Fields of study or special interest:
Business administration, health care administration, and professional arts

Other information:
Degree programs offered through directed independent study with campus-based faculty. There is a three-week summer Residency requirement for the Bachelor's. Only one session is required for graduation but more can be attended for extra credit.

The Master's in health care administration is offered in the same format, with a two-week Residency requirement. (This Master's program is a candidate for accreditation.)

Credit for coursework done elsewhere and degree-related job experience. A maximum of four courses (twelve units) is allowed each semester.

Applicants for Bachelor of Science in Professional Arts must be registered nurses.

Saint Mary-Of-The-Woods College

Accredited Bachelor's in many fields and Master's in pastoral theology with a week or less on campus each year. Only women can earn degrees.

Saint Mary-Of-The-Woods
IN 47876

Telephone: (812) 535-5107   Toll-free phone: (800) 356-2647 (IN only)
Fax number: —   Year established: 1840

Degree levels available: Associate's, Bachelor's, Master's
Key person: Kathi Anderson Harvey, Director of Admissions for Non-Traditional Students
Recognition: Accredited by the North Central Association
Ownership: Nonprofit, church
Residency requirement: One week or less each year

Tuition:
$126 per credit hour

Fields of study or special interest:
Associate's and Bachelor's in many fields including accounting, business administration, English, history, humanities, journalism, management, marketing, paralegal studies, political science, psychology, religion, and social work, and women's studies. Master's in pastoral theology.

Other information:
Degrees are earned through individualized independent study. Students work with an instructor to design a plan of study (course) with very specific goals: what will be learned, how learning will take place, how learning will be evaluated. Close contact is maintained between student and instructor throughout the semester by mail and phone.

Following acceptance, each student must spend two and a half days at a new student residency.

Students are required to come to campus twice a year (for one to two days) to present completed projects and design new ones. (Project here means a combination of all courses for one semester.)

Master's students must spend a week on campus during the summer for two separate courses. Master's students use the same program format as undergraduates, but must also complete a required reading list, a written qualifying exam, and a thesis.

Credit is given for experiential learning. Each student has an advisor who helps to formulate a long-range academic plan.

The college admits men and women to its programs, but only women can earn degrees.

Saybrook Institute

Accredited Master's and Doctorates in psychology and human science through home study, with two weeks a year in San Francisco.

1550 Sutter Street
San Francisco, CA 94109

Telephone: (415) 441-5034
Fax number: —

Toll-free phone: —
Year established: 1970

Degree levels available: Master's, Doctorate
Key person: Chester Gerhardt, Admissions and Records Officer
Recognition: Accredited by the Western Association
Ownership: Nonprofit, independent
Residency requirement: Two weeks a year

Tuition:
$6,500 per year

Fields of study or special interest:
Psychology, human science

Other information:
The Master's and Doctorate are offered only through distance learning. New enrollees attend a five-day program-planning seminar. Twice a year, there is a one-week "national meeting"—a seminar to be attended by students and faculty.

The "At-a-distance" learning format uses learning guides prepared by faculty for each course. Students complete coursework at home. Guides outline expectations of the course, and include written lecture materials prepared by the faculty, as well as reading materials.

Progress is guided by communication with faculty by telephone, mail, and computer telecommunication.

Students may design their own courses as well.

The program includes general studies courses (requirements) and area studies courses (which are not exactly majors; they are "ways to group courses and educational experiences" or perhaps just areas of concentration, such as clinical inquiry, consciousness studies, health studies, organizational inquiry, and systems inquiry).

Degrees can take from two to four years to complete.

The Master's program is not a terminal program; it is designed to be a stepping stone to the Ph.D.

Many well-known psychologists have been associated with Saybrook, including Rollo May, Stanley Krippner, Richard Farson, Nevitt Stanford, and Clark Moustakas.

Saybrook, until 1982, was called the Humanistic Psychology Institute.

School Without a Name

Nonresident MBA, and nonresident B.S. in computer science, from a school that does not yet exist, planned by the author of this book.

School without a name
P.O. Box 1616
Hilo, Hawaii 96721

Telephone: (808) 935-3913
Fax number: (808) 969-7469

Toll-free phone: (800) 367-4456
Year established: 1991

Degree levels available: Bachelor's, Master's
Key person: John Bear
Recognition: See text below
Ownership: Will be proprietary
Residency requirement: No residency required

Tuition:
Not yet established. Probably about $3,000 for complete degree program.

Fields of study or special interest:
Business administration and computer science.

Other information:
The school I run, Greenwich University, has had quite a few inquiries from people who *must* have an accredited degree. The problem is that no recognized accrediting agency will even consider a school that offers external or wholly nonresident Doctoral programs. The only way we could hope for accreditation is to start a new entity, offering only Bachelor's and/or Master's degrees. And that is what we are in the process of doing.

The new school will begin with only two programs: the MBA and the B.S. in computer science. Each will be a highly structured program, consisting of approximately twelve courses, each with text, syllabus, papers, and examinations. Up to half the MBA credits and up to one fourth of the B.S. credits can come from work done prior to enrolling, whether in other schools or through lifetime experience.

Although our sole reason for doing this is to achieve accreditation from a recognized agency within three years, and we think the chances are good, there can, of course, be no guarantee that this will happen.

We are looking for one hundred "charter students" (all right, guinea pigs, if you will), to begin this program during 1991 and 1992. We will offer a most attractive price — and a degree program that at the very worst will be a good, sound one, of the quality of any school in this book — and at best, will end up with recognized accreditation.

At presstime, we had neither a name or literature to send . . . but we fully expect to have both by February, 1991, and I didn't want to miss the opportunity to get in my own book, hence this unusual listing. If this might have interest for you, write to the address above, and we will send you further information.

Skidmore College

Accredited Bachelor's degrees in many subjects by home study, with three very short visits to the campus.

University Without Walls
Saratoga Springs, NY 12866

Telephone: (518) 584-5000
Fax number: (518) 584-3023

Toll-free phone: —
Year established: 1911

Degree levels available: Bachelor's
Key person: Kent H. Jones, Director of Admissions
Recognition: Accredited by Middle States Association
Ownership: Nonprofit, independent
Residency requirement: Short

Tuition:
$1,425 per year

Fields of study or special interest:
More than fifty majors including most traditional liberal arts areas and some professional fields, such as business and human services. Students can devise their own majors as well.

Other information:
Skidmore is one of the pioneers of the nontraditional movement; they have offered a university without walls program since 1970.

There are three on-campus meetings required: admissions interview, a first advising session during which the program is developed, and a degree plan meeting, during which the student's proposed program is reviewed by Skidmore faculty.

Skidmore makes it clear that they hold their graduates to "standards of knowledge, competence, and intellectual attainment which are no less comprehensive and rigorous than those established by traditional . . . programs."

After a degree plan has been completed, the student is required to submit a final project in order to graduate. This project must demonstrate the student's achievements/competence in her or his own field.

No specific courses are offered. Learning takes place through independent study, internships, community engagement, jobs, etc. There is no specified length for learning experiences, or number student must undertake at any time.

Once a student completes a learning experience, the student and advisor evaluate it. Either a supervisor will evaluate and grade the work, or in case of self-directed study, the student writes a substantial paper which is evaluated by a faculty member at Skidmore.

Rumors of a Master's program under development keep surfacing, but the school has no official comment.

Southeastern College of the Assemblies of God

Accredited nonresident Bachelor's and short-residency Master's in various religious fields of study.

1000 Longfellow Boulevard
Lakeland, FL 33801-6099

Telephone: (813) 665-4404
Fax number: —

Toll-free phone: —
Year established: 1935

Degree levels available: Bachelor's, Master's
Key person: Thomas Wilson, Director, Continuing Education
Recognition: Accredited by the Southern Association
Ownership: Nonprofit, church
Residency requirement: No residency required

Tuition:
$2,850 per year

Fields of study or special interest:
Pastoral studies, Christian education, Bible, and missions

Other information:
In their correspondence courses, the student receives a study guide and textbook for each course. Exams are given by proctors, and may be taken locally.

Credit is given for experiential learning. If there is no standard test in a student's area of proficiency, the faculty may devise and administer such a test.

There is also a Theological Seminary Extension Center which offers courses leading to a Master of Arts in Biblical Literature. This does not involve correspondence courses, but rather four one-week sessions on campus each year, with independent study in between.

Southern California University for Professional Studies

Nonresident Associate's, Bachelor's, and Master's in business subjects.

3301 West Lincoln Avenue
Anaheim, CA 92801

Telephone: (714) 952-9090
Fax number: —

Toll-free phone: (800) 227-2877
Year established: 1978

Degree levels available: Associate's, Bachelor's, Master's
Key person: Billie Campbell, Director
Recognition: Unaccredited, state authorized
Ownership: Nonprofit
Residency requirement: No residency required

Tuition:
$360 per course

Fields of study or special interest:
Business administration, paralegal studies (Associate's only)

Other information:
The degrees offered by correspondence study are the Associate of Arts in business or paralegal studies, the Bachelor of Business Administration in either marketing, management, or accounting, and the Master of Business Administration. Courses are offered by mail, phone, and audio tape. Each course may be completed in four to sixteen weeks. For the Master's, forty units of work (ten courses) must be completed after enrolling. Credit is given for other college work, prior learning, and life experience assessment. Challenge exams may be taken in the various courses and if passed, credit is awarded.

In the correspondence courses, the student receives a study guide for each course (textbooks are not included in cost, but can be ordered from their bookstore). These include specific information about the course: chapter assignments and due dates, chapter summaries of textbook, instructor's comments, etc. The student is encouraged to keep in touch with professors by mail and phone. Most courses will include written assignments, a term paper or project, and exams given locally by proctors.

[SEE APPENDIX E REGARDING THE CHANGING SITUATION IN CALIFORNIA.]

# Southwest University

Nonresident Bachelor's, Master's, and Doctorates in various fields.

2200 Veterans Boulevard
Kenner, LA 70062

Telephone: (504) 468-2900
Fax number: —

Toll-free phone: (800) 433-5923
Year established: 1982

Degree levels available: Bachelor's, Master's, Doctorates
Key person: Reg Sheldrick, Ph.D., Administrator
Recognition: Unaccredited, state registered
Ownership: Proprietary
Residency requirement: No residency required

Tuition:
$75 per unit

Fields of study or special interest:
Business administration, psychology, counseling, hypnotherapy, education, hospital administration, health services administration, criminal justice, security administration, computer science, construction management, and engineering management

Other information:
Southwest University was established in 1982 by its president, Dr. Grayce Lee, and Dr. Reg Sheldrick. (Sheldrick also established the school now called Newport University.) Southwest University maintains a curriculum development office in Omaha, Nebraska.

Degree requirements can be satisfied by credit earned at other colleges and universities, credit given for military service/courses, credit for specialized training and experiential learning, and by undertaking independent study courses. All students must complete a final written project: term paper, thesis, dissertation, or research paper.

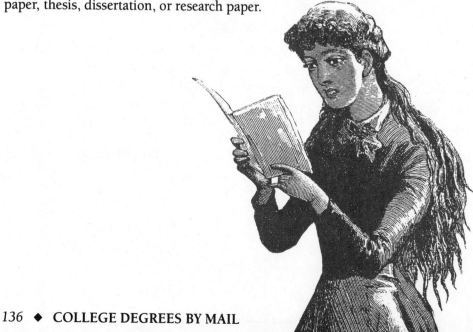

Southwestern Adventist College

Accredited Associate's and Bachelor's degrees in many fields with eleven days on campus the first year, three the second.

Adult Degree Program
Keene, TX 76059

Telephone: (817) 645-2271   Toll-free phone: (800) 433-2240
Fax number: —   Year established: 1893

Degree levels available: Associate's, Bachelor's
Key person: Marie Redwine, Director
Recognition: Accredited by the Southwestern Association
Ownership: Nonprofit, church
Residency requirement: Short

Tuition:
$2,592 per year

Fields of study or special interest:
Business administration, behavioral science, communication, education, English, home economics, mathematics, office administration, physical education, religion, social science, social work, and Spanish

Other information:
They offer a Bachelor of Arts, Science, or Business Administration.

Credit is given for experiential learning (especially as related to work experience), through proficiency exams, transfer of credit, and independent study.

There are correspondence courses, in which students mail in their papers. Instructors are available by mail and phone. Credit may also be earned by television courses and classes at another school if approved by the faculty.

An eight-day admissions seminar on campus is required before starting classes. Seminars are held in April, June, and October. Also required is a three-day on-campus seminar once a year (for many things, including motivation talks and worship time).

At least thirty hours (units) must be earned after enrollment. Adult Degree Plan students pay 80 percent of the tuition of on-campus students.

State University of Florida

Accredited Bachelor's degrees with a minimum of two weeks on campus.

External Degree Program
School of Extended Studies and Learning Technologies
University of South Florida
Tampa, FL 33620

Telephone: (813) 974-4058   Toll-free phone: —
Fax number: —   Year established: 1956

Degree levels available: Bachelor's
Key person: Kevin Kearney, Ph.D., Director
Recognition: Accredited by the Southern Association
Ownership: Nonprofit, state
Residency requirement: Two weeks minimum

Tuition:
$4,843.20 for Florida residents, $15,169 for others

Fields of study or special interest:
Independent studies; no majors offered

Other information:
This statewide program is accessible to students through four schools: University of South Florida (Tampa), Florida State University (Tallahassee), University of Florida (Gainesville), and the University of North Florida (Jacksonville). They hope eventually to involve the other five Universities in Florida's State University Program.

The degree is awarded by University of South Florida.

The program is based on a curriculum of interdisciplinary studies, divided into four study areas: social sciences, natural sciences, humanities, and interarea studies. Pre-enrollees take a series of diagnostic tests to determine knowledge and skills. This information is used as a guide for where to start in the curriculum.

Guided independent study (the tutorial) represents 90 percent of effort in the first three study areas. Students receive an official guide which consists of learning objectives, concept inventories, and reading suggestions for each area (also a "study model" to illustrate how one might proceed). Students interact with a faculty advisor who monitors learning activities until such time as the advisor indicates that the student is ready to sit for a comprehensive exam in that area.

There is a two-week seminar necessary on campus for each area, although each of the first three areas can be waived if there is sufficient prior experience.

A thesis is necessary as part of the fourth study area.

Stephens College

Accredited Bachelor's degrees by home study, requiring two weekends on campus.

College Without Walls
Campus Box 2083
Columbia, MO 65215

Telephone: (314) 876-7125
Fax number: (314) 876-7248

Toll-free phone: (800) 388-7579
Year established: 1833

Degree levels available: Bachelor's
Key person: LuAnna Andrews, New Student Coordinator
Recognition: Accredited by the North Central Association
Ownership: Nonprofit
Residency requirement: Two weekends or eight days

Tuition:
$1,875 for the first year program tuition (mandatory three full courses); $1,250 for annual program tuition thereafter (two courses)

Fields of study or special interest:
Many fields available, but "most SCWW students major in psychology, business, health information management, or early childhood education."

Other information:
Stephens is a woman's college. They offer both on-campus classes and an external degree program of independent study. Forty-three units (not like other schools' units) are required for the degree. Ten must be completed with the Stephens faculty after enrolling.

All students are required to attend a liberal studies seminar before beginning their program, either eight days or two weekends.

At the seminar, students are assigned an advisor who works with them in planning their degree program, and continues to assist them throughout. The plan must fulfill Stephens's degree requirements. Credit is given for experiential learning.

Independent study consists either of guided study (structured course, with syllabus, texts, and assignments) or contract study (student and faculty member [sponsor] design course objectives and content, method of evaluation, amount of credit, and course level).

Summit University

Bachelor's, Master's, and Doctorates entirely through home study.

5703 Read Boulevard
New Orleans, LA 70127

Telephone: (504) 241-0227   Toll-free phone: —
Fax number: —   Year established: 1988

Degree levels available: Bachelor's, Master's, Doctorates
Key person: David L. Schwartz, Trustee
Recognition: Unaccredited, state registered
Ownership: Nonprofit
Residency requirement: No residency is required

Tuition:

—

Fields of study or special interest:
Many fields of study available

Other information:
Summit University declares that they are an "assessment university, critically assessing a person's lifelong learning." In other words, they assess a student's learning rather than teaching him or her anything. "No extraneous courses are required." (Summit does not offer courses.)

Following an evaluation, the university determines how credits earned are to be earned. The student designs her or his own program with adjunct faculty or tutors from another school; the university does not have its own faculty per se. Students work with an RF/ACC (resource faculty/administrative academic counselor) in designing the program.

Students can create their own degree category.

Each student has a trustee to work with throughout the process (to assess, advise, and counsel). The student (with the trustee's assistance) determines what is necessary to complete current studies. Students independently contract with outside mentors. Most learning is documented and credit is earned through writing papers and essays. A major study which adds to human knowledge is required at all degree levels.

After one has paid tuition for three years (two at the Master's level), no further tuition is required.

The address is a mail-forwarding service. There is no connection with the Summit University that has operated from California and Idaho, nor the seminary of that name in Indiana.

Syracuse University

Accredited Bachelor's, M.B.A., Master of Fine Arts (advertising, illustration), M.A. in food management, and more, with as little as three weeks on campus.

Independent Study Degree Programs
610 East Fayette Street
Syracuse, NY 13244

Telephone: (315) 423-3284   Toll-free phone: —
Fax number: (315) 443-1954   Year established: 1870

Degree levels available: Bachelor's, Master's
Key person: Robert Colley, Director
Recognition: Accredited by the Middle States Association
Ownership: Nonprofit, independent
Residency requirement: Two or three weeks a year

Tuition:
$199 per credit for undergraduate work, $325 per credit for graduate

Fields of study or special interest:
Business administration, food systems management, fine arts (advertising), social science, liberal studies

Other information:
The Bachelor's degrees and the M.B.A. require one week on campus at the beginning of each trimester (that is, three weeks a year). The other Master's degrees require a two-week residence during the summer.

The M.F.A., specializing in advertising graphics and illustration, has been taught by many of New York advertising's best-known art directors (Lubalin, Scali, Gargano, etc.). It also requires several shorter sessions a year in New York city and other metropolitan areas.

The social science program is also offered in London.

During the other forty-nine or fifty weeks of the year, correspondence courses are available, consisting of required reading, assignments, and regular contact with professors through telephone, fax, and electronic mail.

Credit for experiential learning is available only for the Bachelor's programs.

The minimum time for the Bachelor's degree is one year (thirty credits) for people with substantial transfer credit, but in practice, most people take quite a bit longer than that.

Thomas Edison State College

Accredited Associate's and Bachelor's in many fields, entirely by correspondence or over a home computer.

101 West State Street
Trenton, NJ 08625

Telephone: (609) 984-1150   Toll-free phone: —
Fax number: (609) 984-1193   Year established: 1972

Degree levels available: Associate's, Bachelor's
Key person: Jack Phillips, Registrar
Recognition: Accredited by the Middle States Association
Ownership: Nonprofit, state
Residency requirement: No residency required

Tuition:

Annual enrollment fee: $200 (non–New Jersey: $350).
 Credit evaluation fee, dependent on number of credits: $25–$300 (non-NJ: $50–$600)
 Guided study per credit: $35 (non-New Jersey: $50). Each challenge exam: $25 (non–New Jersey: $35). A Bachelor's will probably be in the range of $2,000 to $3,000.

Fields of study or special interest:

Almost any field

Other information:

Bachelor of Science in business administration, applied science and technology, human services, or nursing; Bachelor of Arts in any of twenty-six subjects, entirely by nonresident study. (Nursing degrees are for New Jersey residents only.)
 Advisors are available by telephone; also, there are counseling centers in various New Jersey cities, but it is not necessary to visit them.
 Credit is given for experiential knowledge (portfolio assessment; a handbook is available), transfer credit from accredited colleges, training programs, etc. Once prior credit has been evaluated, an advisor helps students design a course of study to complete the degree.
 The degree plan may include credit for: independent study (validated by exam or assessment), exams (Edison has their own in dozens of subjects), training programs (military, business, and industry), equivalency exams (over four hundred available), guided study (available through Edison, these correspondence courses incorporate reading, written assignments, study guides, and possibly videotapes and television programs), and courses from other schools (both on-campus and correspondence), telecourses, and Computer Facilitated Learning (CFL student communicates with a mentor by computer. Mentor provides readings, assignments, and evaluations).
 Degrees can be earned over home computers through Electronic University.
 Edison's catalog is a model of clarity and useful information.

 Troy State University

Accredited Associate's and Bachelor's in many fields entirely through home study.

Whitley Hall
P.O. Box 4419
Montgomery, AL 36103

Telephone: (205) 241-9553
Fax number: (205) 793-7951

Toll-free phone: —
Year established: 1887

Degree levels available: Associate's, Bachelor's
Key person: JoEllen Carlson, Ph.D., Director, External Degree Programs
Recognition: Accredited by the Southern Association
Ownership: Nonprofit, state
Residency requirement: No residency is required

Tuition:
Cost per quarter hour (192 necessary for degree)
   On-campus and TV courses, $28; learning contracts, $42 for Alabamans, $62 for others

Fields of study or special interest:
Associate's in general education; Bachelor's in professional studies (concentration in resources management, criminal justice, English, history, political science, psychology, or sociology)

Other information:
Persons living within two hundred miles of Montgomery must attend a short orientation session on the campus. For those living farther away this can be done by mail.

Students may get credit from Troy State residential courses, Troy State learning contracts for distance learning, Troy State television courses (on PBS), courses at other accredited universities (both on-campus and correspondence). Each student must also complete a senior project.

Faculty have developed learning contracts that closely parallel requirements in University resident courses. They are available for most courses. Students may also design their own learning contracts with the guidance and assistance of Troy State faculty.

No correspondence courses are offered, but they can be taken at other schools for Troy State credit. Credit for life experience is available, but only after a student has completed a course in this subject.

The minimum residency is thirty-six quarter hours (roughly six months) for the Bachelor's and thirty-five for the Master's.

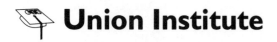 # Union Institute

A rare opportunity to earn an accredited Ph.D. in many fields primarily (not entirely) by home study. Not fast, not cheap, but very well regarded.

440 East McMillan Street
Cincinnati, OH 45206-1947

Telephone: (513) 861-6400
Fax number: (513) 651-2310

Toll-free phone: (800) 543-0366
Year established: 1964

Degree levels available: Bachelor's, Doctorates
Key person: Jennifer King-Cooper, Ph.D., Coordinator of Graduate Admissions
Recognition: Accredited by the North Central Association
Ownership: Nonprofit, independent
Residency requirement: Short

Tuition:
$1,821 per quarter for undergraduates, $2,106 per quarter for graduate students

Fields of study or special interest:
Many fields

Other information:
Established by the Union for Experimenting Colleges and Universities (hence the name), a consortium including some large state universities, to be, in effect, their alternative program.

Students must attend an orientation colloquium held in various locations (ten days for Doctorate, a weekend for the Bachelor's). Bachelor's students must attend occasional seminars. Doctoral students must attend at least three five-day seminars, and another ten days of local meetings with three or more students. Thus the total "residency" for the Ph.D. is thirty-five days.

Union does not admit students on a part-time basis. Full-time means at least twelve credits per quarter. At least nine months are required to complete the Bachelor's, and two to four years (the upper end is more common) for the Doctorate; thus the Doctoral cost can easily exceed $25,000.

The Doctoral student develops a committee of at least five, including two experts and two peers. The committee establishes a learning agreement, including an internship, and a "project demonstrating excellence."

The Bachelor's student plans a degree program with an advisor. Credit is earned through various means under the guidance of a faculty sponsor. The undergraduate "University Without Walls" Bachelor's degree may involve independent study, directed reading, internships, on-the-job education, classroom instruction, tutorials, etc., plus a senior thesis, including an oral presentation to a degree review committee.

Union has begun offering their undergraduate degree program "at the facilities of major corporations throughout the United States." Former name: Union Graduate School, until 1990.

# University of Alabama

Accredited Bachelor's in many fields with two days on campus, and a Master's in criminal justice with two weeks on campus.

New College External Degree Program
P.O. Box 870182
Tuscaloosa, AL 35487

Telephone: (205) 348-6000
Fax number: (205) 348-6544

Toll-free phone: —
Year established: 1831

Degree levels available: Bachelor's
Key person: Dr. Harriet Cabell, Director, External Degree Program
Recognition: Accredited by the Southern Association
Ownership: Nonprofit, state
Residency requirement: Two days on campus

Tuition:
$68 per semester hour

Fields of study or special interest:
Human services, humanities, social sciences, natural sciences, applied sciences, administrative sciences, and communication

Other information:
The degrees of Bachelor of Arts and Bachelor of Science may be earned entirely through nonresident independent study with the exception of a degree-planning seminar at the start of the program. Students are required to attend one two-and-a-half-day seminar on campus prior to admission.

Credit may be earned for on-campus courses, out-of-class learning contracts (independent study), correspondence courses, television courses, Weekend College, and credit for prior learning.

Academic planning and advising is conducted by telephone and written correspondence.

Students don't complete a traditional major, but do choose an area of concentration in an interdisciplinary field of study.

At least thirty-two hours of work must be completed after enrolling at the university. A twelve-semester-hour senior project is required of all students. There often seems to be a waiting list to get into this program.

The Tuscaloosa campus of the University offers a Master's in Criminal Justice, requiring two weeks on campus. Information from the College of Continuing Studies, Box 2967, Tuscaloosa, AL 35486.

University of Durham

British M.B.A. almost entirely through correspondence study.

Old Shire Hall, Old Elvet
Durham DH1 3HP, England

Telephone: (0385) 64466   **Toll-free phone:** —
Fax number: —   **Year established:** 1988 (this program)

Degree levels available: Master's
Key person: Registrar
Recognition: Equivalent of accredited
Ownership: Nonprofit, state
Residency requirement: Very short residency

Tuition:
£5,500 (about $8,000)

Fields of study or special interest:
Business administration

Other information:
In 1988, Durham, one of the long-established major British universities, introduced a distance learning M.B.A. The actual study for the degree is administered by non-degree-granting Rapid Results College (Tuition House, 27/37 St George's Road, London, SW19 4DS England, Phone (01) 947-2211), which specializes in coursework preparing students for various university examinations. The approach is comparable to that offered by the University of Warwick through Rapid Results College's rival, Wolsey Hall.

The degree program typically requires four years to complete, with the possibility of brief required periods of study (a week or so) on the campus in England, or at centers in various Asian locations. Examinations are required at regular intervals, which may be taken locally under supervision. Midway through the program, one receives a Certificate in Business Administration.

# University of Iowa

Accredited Bachelor of Liberal Studies entirely through home study.

Center for Credit Programs
Division of Continuing Education
116 International Center
Iowa City, IA 52242

Telephone: (319) 335-2575   Toll-free phone: (800) 553-IOWA
Fax number: —   Year established: 1847

Degree levels available: Bachelor's
Key person: Scot Wilcox, Educational Advisor
Recognition: Accredited by the North Central Association
Ownership: Nonprofit, state
Residency requirement: No residency is required

Tuition:
$55 per semester hour for guided correspondence study

Fields of study or special interest:
Liberal studies

Other information:
The Bachelor of Arts in liberal studies can be earned entirely by correspondence from the University of Iowa and the University of Northern Iowa.

There are no majors in the program, but students must earn twelve credits in three of these five areas: humanities, communication and arts, science and math, social sciences, and professional fields (business, education, etc.).

Credit is also earned through guided correspondence study courses. Students mail in assignments and take proctored exams. Credit can also be earned through on-campus evening and weekend courses, televised courses, off-campus course sites throughout Iowa, courses from other regionally accredited four-year colleges (both on-campus and correspondence), and telebridge courses. "Telebridge" is a statewide system of two-way audio conferencing which permits classes to be held at remote locations. No credit is given for life experience.

To qualify for admission, a student must live in the United States and have completed sixty-two transferable units or have an Associate's degree. At least forty-five semester hours must be earned at the Iowa Regents Universities (University of Iowa, Iowa State University, University of Northern Iowa).

# University of London

Accredited nonresident Bachelor's, Master's, and Doctorates in a variety of fields from the school that invented the whole concept.

Senate House
Malet Street
London WC1E 7HU England

Telephone: (01) 636-8000	Toll-free phone: —
Fax number: —	Year established: 1836

Degree levels available: Bachelor's, Master's, Doctorates
Key person: Andrea Kelly, Deputy Secretary for External Students
Recognition: Equivalent of accredited in England
Ownership: Nonprofit
Residency requirement: No residency is required

Tuition:
Cost varies according to degree program and also whether taken in the UK or overseas; the range is from £600 to £1,500 (roughly $900 to $2,400)

Fields of study or special interest:
Many fields including religious studies, music, agriculture, nursing, law (67 percent of enrollment)

Other information:
London was the world's first external degree program, and after a century and a half, it is still among the best. They do have an annoying policy that only holders of their own Bachelor's can enroll in the Doctoral (and with few exceptions, in the Master's) programs. Anyone may apply directly for the Master's in agricultural development, French studies, and classics.

There are new programs in accounting, banking, management, and nursing, with agrarian development and computer science under development.

Degrees are based solely on exams and a thesis. Students are "responsible for deciding for themselves the way in which they prepare for examinations."

The external program encompasses a system of independent guided study in certain subjects. They provide reading lists and past examination papers, and in some cases subject guides, occasional short courses, and informal tutorial assessment (of essays, etc.) Optional correspondence and audio-visual materials have been made available.

Students can take exams at centers in most countries around the world (at British embassies and consulates). One is allowed four attempts at each exam to be taken.

Minimum period of study for a Bachelor's degree is three years. This is inflexible, as is the requirement that you must have *their* Bachelor's (even if you have a Harvard or Oxford Master's) before doing a Doctorate.

Research degrees (M.Phil. and Ph.D.) are only available to graduates of U. of London.

Only graduates of universities in the U.K. may apply for the external law degree.

Several correspondence schools offer nondegree preparation for London's exams. One is Wolsey Hall, 66 Banbury, Oxford OX2 6PR; another is Rapid Results College, Tuition House, London SW19 3BR.

University of Maryland

Accredited Bachelor's degrees by home study, with a few short visits to the campus in Maryland.

University College, Open Learning Program
University Boulevard at Adelphi Road
College Park, MD 20742

Telephone: (301) 985-7722
Fax number: (301) 454-0399

Toll-free phone: (800) 888-UMEC
Year established: 1856

Degree levels available: Bachelor's
Key person: William Wolff, Assistant Dean, Open Learning Program
Recognition: Accredited by the Middle States Association
Ownership: Nonprofit, state
Residency requirement: A few short visits to campus

Tuition:
$117 per credit hour

Fields of study or special interest:
Technology and management, behavioral and social sciences, humanities, fire science

Other information:
University College, the continuing education campus of the University of Maryland, offers Bachelor of Arts and Bachelor of Science degrees in a flexible format through its Open Learning Program. Attendance is optional except for the introductory session and examinations.

Learning centers exist throughout the Washington-Baltimore area. Primary concentrations are in technology and management, behavioral and social sciences, and the humanities. A primary concentration in fire science is offered through independent study in a six-state region and the District of Columbia. University College also offers a primary concentration in Paralegal Studies in an independent study format.

Credit is available for relevant college-level prior learning.

The university offers its own correspondence classes (some with video cassettes) with instructors available by mail and phone.

University of Missouri–Columbia

Accredited Bachelor of Science in agriculture, entirely by home study.

Nontraditional Study Programs
103 Whitten Hall
Columbia, MO 65211

Telephone: (314) 882-6287   Toll-free phone: —
Fax number: (314) 882-6957   Year established: 1839

Degree levels available: Bachelor's
Key person: Greg Nolting, Director, Nontraditional Study Program
Recognition: Accredited by the North Central Association
Ownership: Nonprofit, state
Residency requirement: Very short

Tuition:
$1,806 per year

Fields of study or special interest:
Agriculture

Other information:
The Bachelor of Science in agriculture is available entirely by correspondence study. Students complete their courses at their own pace working at home. Faculty/student contact is maintained by telephone.

Each student's progress is monitored by the program director and advice is provided by a faculty committee.

The program is designed for those who have interrupted their college education and cannot return to campus. In general, individuals whose education has been interrupted for five or more years are eligible for the program. Priority is given to those who have completed most of the general education requirements for a Bachelor's degree, but one can apply even if one has no college experience at all.

Credit is earned through coursework at college, correspondence courses, extension courses, departmental examinations, experiential learning (documented by exams, a portfolio of prior learning, or other acceptable means), and special projects directed by a University faculty advisor.

The program is not available to persons outside the United States.

 # University of Oklahoma

Accredited Bachelor's and Master's in liberal studies, with a total of two to seven weeks on campus in Oklahoma.

College of Liberal Studies
1700 Asp Avenue, Suite 226
Norman, OK 73037

Telephone: (405) 325-1061
Fax number: —

Toll-free phone: (800) 522-4389
Year established: 1890

Degree levels available: Bachelor's, Master's
Key person: Konnie Hall, Coordinator, Student Information
Recognition: Accredited by the North Central Association
Ownership: Nonprofit, state
Residency requirement: Short

Tuition:
Bachelor's: $3,410 for residents, $6,700 for out of state; Master's: $1,635 for residents, $3,200 for out of state

Fields of study or special interest:
Liberal studies

Other information:
The College of Liberal Studies was established in 1960, making it one of the real pioneers in this field. There are no majors; students do elective study based on their interests. Work is done through a combination of guided independent study based on a faculty/student tutorial relationship and short-term intensive seminars on the University of Oklahoma campus.

Bachelor's students complete studies in four areas. The first three are: humanities, natural sciences, and social sciences. The final area integrates the previous three, and the student completes a study in depth. Each area takes up to a year and is worth thirty units. Any or all of the first three areas can be waived, either based on prior study or by passing an examination.

There is an Upper Division Option for people with two years of college. It begins with a five-day residential seminar, then completion of the first three phases in about a year, with one required seminar. The final seminar is the same as in the four-year program.

Grading for study phases is based on comprehensive exams, which may be taken at college or locally, supervised by a proctor.

The Bachelor's curriculum consists of core study from reading lists developed by the faculty, learning contracts allowing students to focus on a topic of particular interest, and a senior thesis.

The Master of Liberal Studies is largely for people with a specialized Bachelor's who wish a broader education. It requires two two-week seminars and one three-week colloquium.

The Master's program is based on an individualized study program/plan developed by the student and advisors, culminating in the writing and presentation of a thesis.

University of Santa Barbara

Master's and Doctorates in education and business by home study, with a minimum of three weeks on campus in California.

4050 Calle Real, Suite 200
Santa Barbara, CA 93110

Telephone: (805) 569-1024   Toll-free phone: —
Fax number: —   Year established: 1973

Degree levels available: Master's, Doctorates
Key person: Julia Reinhart Coburn, Ph.D., President
Recognition: Unaccredited, state-approved
Ownership: Nonprofit, independent
Residency requirement: Minimum of three weeks

Tuition:

—

Fields of study or special interest:
Education, business administration, human behavior, international studies

Other information:
The university offers the M.A. and the Ph.D. in education and the Doctor of Education, with emphasis in education, counseling psychology, business and finance, or international studies, as they relate to the field of education.

The programs require a minimum of three weeks residency in Santa Barbara. Degrees require one to three years to complete. The twelve resident faculty and more than fifty nonresident advisors all have traditional Doctorates.

U.S.B. offers both independent study and correspondence study in many aspects of the field of education, including counseling psychology. Candidates for the degree must complete courses and independent study work, and pass an examination in each study area.

Students may contribute to the design of their programs of study within the parameters of the specified degree program and in consultation with a faculty advisor.

Resident classes and special seminars are offered at designated times throughout the year.

The university has extension programs in Hong Kong, Taiwan, and Thailand.

Originally established in Florida as Laurence University.

[SEE APPENDIX E REGARDING THE CHANGING SITUATION IN CALIFORNIA.]

 # University of Sarasota

Accreditation candidate. Programs offering the M.B.A. and Doctorates in education by home study plus six weeks in Florida.

950 South Tamiami Trail
Sarasota, FL 34236

Telephone: (813) 355-2906   Toll-free phone: (800) 331-5995
Fax number: —   Year established: 1969

Degree levels available: Bachelor's, Master's, Doctorates
Key person: Dr. Robert Zeller, President
Recognition: Candidate for accreditation with the Southern Association
Ownership: Nonprofit
Residency requirement: Short

Tuition:
$225 per credit hour

Fields of study or special interest:
Business, education

Other information:
Master of Business Administration, Master of Arts in education, and Doctor of Education. Some intensive coursework in Florida is required. Courses are in the summer, with one-week seminars in winter and spring. Total residency may be as short as six weeks. The university's programs consist of seminars, supervised individual research, and writing, combined with the residential sessions.

Master's candidates either write a thesis or complete a directed independent study project. Doctoral students must write a dissertation. Many of the students are teachers and school administrators. Originally known as Laurence University, the predecessor of the Laurence University that opened in California and is now the University of Santa Barbara.

University of South Africa

Accredited nonresident Bachelor's, Master's, and Doctorates in many fields from the largest correspondence university in the English-speaking world.

P.O. Box 392
Pretoria, 0001 South Africa

Telephone: (012) 429-4116   Toll-free phone: —
Fax number: —   Year established: 1910

Degree levels available: Bachelor's, Master's, Doctorates
Key person: Registrar
Recognition: Equivalent of accredited, in South Africa
Ownership: Nonprofit, state
Residency requirement: No residency required

Tuition:
The cost of the programs, government subsidized, is very low.

Fields of study or special interest:
Many fields

Other information:
The University of South Africa, known as UNISA, offers Bachelor's, Master's and Doctorates entirely by correspondence study (with the exception of final exams, which may be taken in cities with South African embassy and consular offices worldwide). The model is quite similar to the University of London, but unlike London, South Africa does not require that you earn *their* Bachelor's before going on for higher degrees.

All work is by correspondence study. Printed study guides are sent to the student, as well as supplementary material (tapes, etc.), and recommended texts. Students remain in contact with instructors by mail or personal interview (phone calls are discouraged).

Lectures and discussion groups are held at various centers in South Africa throughout the year. They are recommended, but not mandatory.

Students pursuing some degrees, at some levels, may be asked to attend a residential session of one to three weeks.

A minimum of ten courses is required for the Bachelor's degree, and the minimum time is three years.

Before registering, one must obtain a Certificate of Full or Conditional Exemption from the South African Matriculation Examinations, obtained from the Matriculation Board, P.O. Box 3854, Pretoria, South Africa, 0001. Ask for a certificate to register at UNISA. People worldwide are admitted, primarily if they can show that it is difficult or impossible for them to pursue the degree where they are, whether for reasons of isolation, subject matter, time, or money.

Some people have had reservations about dealing with a South African school, especially before the political and social changes that began in 1989. UNISA points proudly to the many thousands of black Africans currently enrolled, and that people like Nelson Mandela and Dr. Robert Mugabe of Zimbabwe studied there.

University of the State of New York

Accredited Bachelor of Arts and Bachelor of Science entirely through nonresidential study at America's oldest chartered state university.

Regents College
1450 Western Avenue
Albany, NY 12230

Telephone: (518) 474-3703
Fax number: —

Toll-free phone: —
Year established: 1784

Degree levels available: Associate's, Bachelor's
Key person: C. Wayne Williams, Executive Director
Recognition: Accredited by the Middle States Association
Ownership: Nonprofit, state
Residency requirement: No residency required

Tuition:
Enrollment fee: $375; Annual advising/evaluation fee: $200

Fields of study or special interest:
Liberal arts, business, nursing, technology

Other information:
The Bachelor of Arts and Bachelor of Science can be earned entirely by nonresidential study. Probably the largest and, along with Thomas Edison State College, the most popular nonresident degree program in the U.S.

The oldest state educational agency in America has no faculty, no campus, and no courses of its own. It evaluates work done elsewhere, and awards its own degrees to persons who have accumulated sufficient units, by whatever means.

Credit is given for all prior college courses and many noncollege learning experiences (company courses, military, etc.). The university recognizes many equivalency exams and offers its own as well, given nationwide and, by arrangement, at foreign locations. Each degree has its own requirements with regard to area of emphasis; however, they are not restrictive. They require a minimum number of units in the arts and sciences.

The program is described in a twenty-four-page viewbook, sent free to all who request it. If nonschool learning experiences cannot be assessed easily at a distance, or by exam, the student may go to New York for an oral examination. The university makes available a service called DISTANCE-LEARN, which is a computer database of courses offered by other schools that can be completed through home study.

Potential students should be cautioned that there are many groups, especially in nursing, representing themselves as Regents College's agents or claiming to have a relationship with them. These groups are not sanctioned by the college. Students are encouraged to contact the college directly.

 # University of Wales

Accredited Doctorates mostly by home study, with short visits to Wales from time to time.

The Registrar of the University of Wales
University Registry
Cathays Park
Cardiff CF1 3NS Wales, United Kingdom

Telephone: (0222) 382656   Toll-free phone: —
Fax number: —   Year established: —

Degree levels available: Doctorates
Key person: The Registrar
Recognition: Equivalent of accredited in United Kingdom
Ownership: Nonprofit, state
Residency requirement: No residency required

Tuition:
Modest fees

Fields of study or special interest:
Almost any field

Other information:
In addition to the traditional residential approaches, students of the five constituent colleges of the University of Wales may earn the Ph.D. by pursuing full-time research or part-time research externally, in the place of employment or elsewhere. The student begins by enrolling in one of the colleges. Enrollment must be for three years, or nine terms, the first year of which is considered a probationary period, except for persons with approved Master's or sufficient career experience.

Degree candidates are supervised by a faculty member of the college, or of an affiliated school. The student's employer must confirm that the student will be working (full or part time) on a particular research topic. A supervisor is also appointed at the place of employment.

After the dissertation is submitted and read, there is an oral examination of the candidate, following which either the degree is granted, the student is asked to modify the dissertation, or the degree is refused.

If the student can only pursue the necessary dissertation research part time, then he or she must be enrolled for fifteen terms instead of nine, but the other rules remain the same.

While there is no residency required on campus, students must work out with their academic supervisor a satisfactory plan for keeping in touch. Typically, this will mean several visits a year, or one period of extended stay on campus (up to a month).

The constituent colleges: University College of Wales, Aberystwyth, Dyfed SY23 2AX (phone 0970-623177); University College of North Wales, Bangor, Gwynedd LL57 2DG (phone 0248-351151); University of Wales College of Cardiff, Box 78, Cardiff CF1 1XL (phone 0222 874000); University College of Swansea, Singleton Park, Swansea SA2 8PP (phone 0792-205678), St. David's University College, Lampeter, Dyfed SA48 7ED (phone 0570-422351).

University of Warwick

Accredited British M.B.A. through home study, with three eight-day sessions on campus in England or Hong Kong.

Distance Learning M.B.A. Program
Warwick Business School
Coventry, CV4 7AL England

Telephone: (0203) 524100
Fax number: —

Toll-free phone: —
Year established: 1965

Degree levels available: Master's
Key person: Dr. Roy Johnston, Director, Distance Learning M.B.A. Programme
Recognition: Equivalent of accreditation in England
Ownership: Nonprofit
Residency requirement: Twenty-four days

Tuition:
£4,780 (about $7,000)

Fields of study or special interest:
Business

Other information:
Students anywhere in the world may register with Warwick, and then pursue the M.B.A. from home, with the aid of a distance learning course developed by Wolsey Hall, a private school that has for many years offered distance learning courses for the University of London's external degrees.

Students are required to attend an eight-day seminar at Warwick (or at their Hong Kong office) each September, before beginning each of the three parts of the program. Optional weekend seminars are held at Warwick, Hong Kong, Malaysia, and Singapore three times a year.

Access to a computer is recommended but not essential.

Primary work is a program of completing assignments at the rate of two per month. Each student is assigned a tutor for each course who corrects work and is available by phone. Tutors come from the Warwick staff or "another institution of higher education."

Exams are held regularly at Warwick, Hong Kong, and Singapore. Special arrangements can be made for exams in other countries. (Exams are held in as many as thirty countries each year.)

The program has three parts. Parts A and B cover core ideas and "tools" needed in business. Part C gives student choice in electives, to go in depth in area of interest. At end of A, B, & C, a dissertation is written.

The period of study is normally four years, roughly twelve hours a week, but it can be three years if the dissertation is completed during the final year of study.

Wolsey Hall also offers a free six-lesson course in essential study skills, for those who have been away from learning for a while.

 # University of Waterloo

Accredited Bachelor's degrees entirely through home study, primarily but not exclusively for Canadians.

Correspondence Program
Waterloo, Ontario N2L 3G1 Canada

Telephone: (519) 888-4050   Toll-free phone: —
Fax number: —   Year established: 1960

Degree levels available: Bachelor's
Key person: Bruce A. Lumsden, Associate Director for Distance Education
Recognition: Equivalent of accreditation in Canada
Ownership: Nonprofit
Residency requirement: No residency required

Tuition:
$184 per course

Fields of study or special interest:
Many fields

Other information:
The programs are available to people in Canada and the United States, but U.S. students pay three to four times the tuition of Canadians, and the university is not very enthusiastic about the prospect of U.S. students. They write, "experience has proved it is not advisable for U.S. students to enroll in our courses." They also point out that "the rigid nature of program (very fixed assignment and exam schedule) inherent problems with postal system and customs makes it hard to meet time requirements."

If a person in the U.S. *really* wants to do this, in spite of the resistance, one suggestion: There are six assignments per course; it might well be worth the expense of sending them via Federal Express.

The Bachelor's degrees include a nonmajor B.A., a B.A. with a major in classical civilization, economics, English, geography, history, philosophy, psychology, sociology, or social development studies; a Bachelor of Environmental Studies in geography; and a Bachelor of Science in general science.

Credit is given for prior academic experience, but no credit is given for experiential learning.

Correspondence study includes audio (and some video) tapes and course notes sent to students. Students send assignments back to the school at the rate of two a month. Students may communicate with instructors of courses by letter or phone. Many instructors have specific "telephone hours."

Exams are given on a Saturday at the end of each term. There are many exam centers (about one hundred) throughout Canada. Any student who lives more than eighty kilometers from a center may arrange for a proctored exam.

Upper Iowa University

Accredited Bachelor's degree in business subjects by home study with two or four weeks on campus in Iowa.

Box 1861
Fayette, IA 52142

Telephone: (319) 425-5200   Toll-free phone: 800-632-5954 (IA)
                                                    (800) 553-4150 (elsewhere)

Fax number: (319) 425-5271   Year established: 1857

Degree levels available: Bachelor's
Key person: David Fritz, Dean of Continuing Education
Recognition: Accredited by North Central Association
Ownership: Nonprofit, independent
Residency requirement: Two or four weeks

Tuition:
$88 per semester hour (30 semester hours of the required 120 earned after enrolling)

Fields of study or special interest:
B.S. in accounting, management, marketing, public administration

Other information:
To earn the Bachelor's degree, students entering the program with sixty or more semester units must spend one two-week session on campus. Those with fewer than sixty units must attend two two-week sessions.

Study takes place through correspondence courses using learning modules containing a syllabus, texts, and assignments sent to the student. Frequent contact is maintained between the student and professors through mail and telephone. All courses require proctored exams.

Credit is given for experiential learning, as well as previous college work and job training.

Vermont College of Norwich University

Accredited Bachelor's and Master's through home study and either on-campus sessions or meetings with local faculty around the U.S.

College Street
Montpelier, VT 05663

Telephone: (802) 828-8500

Toll-free phone: (800) 553-3326 (VT)
(800) 332-1987 (elsewhere)

Fax number: (802) 223-8855

Year established: 1834

Degree levels available: Bachelor's, Master's
Key person: Kelley Hunter, Assistant Director of Admissions
Recognition: Accredited by New England Association
Ownership: Nonprofit, independent
Residency requirement: Short

Tuition:
$5,670 per year for Bachelor's, $7,350 per year for Master's

Fields of study or special interest:
Many fields (self-designed fields of study), specialized degree programs offered: Master of Fine Arts in writing, Master of Arts in art therapy and Russian

Other information:
All faculty for the Bachelor's program are based at Vermont College and these programs require brief on-campus residencies (nine days every six months or six weekends each semester). Graduate Program faculty are based in major cities around the country and convene their students for area meetings regularly.

The Alternative Education Division includes the undergraduate level Adult Degree program (ADP) and the Graduate Program, offering the M.A. in art therapy, the Master of Fine Arts in writing, and a self-designed M.A. available in counseling, education, and other fields.

Credit is given for experiential learning

Most of the work is done through independent study. One independent study project is done per semester, earning fifteen units. Students have a faculty advisor who helps create a study plan for each semester and supervises the program. The program is designed to allow the students great latitude in designing their study projects. Advisor's "instruction and guidance" is communicated in monthly responses to the student's work.

Russian is only offered as a summer program. It takes three summers to get an M.A.

Norwich entered the nontraditional field in 1981 by acquiring some programs from the then financially strapped Goddard College.

Villarreal National University

You don't often get to yell "Stop the press" in the book publishing world, but I did it here, minutes before this edition went into production.

In 1988, one of the largest universities in Peru began offering nonresident Master's and Doctoral programs, in English, to people living in the U.S. and elsewhere. In my writings, I enthusiastically reported on this unusual development, following several communications from the Rector (President) in Lima.

Literally an hour before this printing of my book was to go into production, details of a fascinating saga became known to me. I actually had the opportunity to phone the good people at Ten Speed and yell, "Stop the press!"

In 1991, Villarreal's office moved from California to Louisiana. In late February, 1991, when I telephoned the number Villarreal provided to its students, the phone was answered "Somerset University." (See page 176.) When an administrator with the Board of Regents of Louisiana telephoned the school in March, 1991 to ask why they had not registered with his office, as the law requires, he was told that the person in charge was Dr. Raymond Young, founder of Somerset, the nonexistent Harley University, and several other schools. These developments were cause for concern.

A lengthy telephone call to Peru in mid March, 1991, produced the following startling information:

1. No one at Villarreal's office in Peru was aware of any U.S. operation.

2. In fact, they all adamantly denied that there was, or could be, any U.S. operation.

3. The address and phone provided to students and to me by Rector Zegarra is *not* the address of Villarreal University.

4. The bursar in Peru stated that the University did not have any bank accounts in the United States, but there *is* an account under that name at the Whitney National Bank in Louisiana, into which U.S. students' tuition checks have been deposited.

5. A person identified in Villarreal's U.S. literature as W. F. Diaz, Assistant to the Rector, is not known to any of the authorities in Peru.

6. Most tellingly, Rector Cotillo Zegarra has "stepped down" recently, and is no longer Rector of the university. The reasons for this action were not announced.

So, what do we have? Dozens, perhaps hundreds of well-meaning students enrolling in a U.S.-based program, apparently unknown to university people in Peru, other than to Rector Cotillo Zegarra, who has just "stepped down." Was Rector Zegarra, with Mr. Diaz and American colleagues, operating a "sideline" unbeknownst to his university? Has a million dollars or more in tuition not found its way to the Villarreal bank account in Peru? Have a goodly number of Americans and Canadians paid well for and "earned" a degree that may be of little use? I don't have any answers yet, but inevitably I will. If you don't want to wait for the next edition of this book, you could send me a self-addressed stamped envelope, marked "Villarreal" and I will send you an update on this situation, as it unfolds. (See page 167.)

# Walden University

Accredited Doctorates in education and management, requiring one three-week summer session plus a few short local weekends.

Institute for Advanced Studies
415 1st Avenue North
Minneapolis, MN 55401

Telephone: (612) 338-7224
Fax number: (612) 338-5092

Toll-free phone: —
Year established: 1970

Degree levels available: Doctorates
Key person: J. Bruce Francis, Vice President for Academic Affairs
Recognition: Accredited by North Central Association
Ownership: Proprietary
Residency requirement: Three-week summer session

Tuition:
$8,780 per year

Fields of study or special interest:
Administration/management, education (Ph.D. and Ed.D.), health services, human services

Other information:
The main residential requirement for Walden's doctoral programs is attendance at a three-week summer session held in Minnesota or, occasionally, at other locations. There is also a short admissions workshop, and two "regional intensive" weekends held in various locations around the country each year. Admissions workshops have been held in a dozen or more cities in the U.S. and Canada each year.

The program is designed for people with Master's degrees and at least three years of professional experience.

Each Walden student demonstrates competence in the knowledge of a Doctoral track by an individualized study plan within a curriculum developed by Walden faculty. The curriculum consists of four core knowledge area modules and three advanced knowledge area modules. (Knowledge area modules cover topics ranging from research methodology to social systems.)

Students are evaluated for knowledge in each module by assignments based on readings, which are evaluated by designated faculty members.

Knowledge area modules include curriculum guides (primary readings, basic concepts and theories) which the student builds upon and uses to identify particular interests.

Students also conduct a research study and write a dissertation based on it. Each student is guided by a faculty advisor, with a reader and external consultant/examiner added at the dissertation stage. Ed.D. candidates must complete a two-hundred-hour supervised internship.

Walden received its accreditation in 1990.

Washington School of Law

Nonresident Master's and Doctorates in taxation for CPAs, lawyers and other businesspeople.

Washington Institute for Graduate Studies
2268 East Newcastle Drive
Salt Lake City, UT 84093

Telephone: (801) 943-2440
Fax number: —

Toll-free phone: —
Year established: 1976

Degree levels available: Master's, Doctorates
Key person: Gary James Joslin, Director of the Graduate Tax Program
Recognition: Unaccredited, state registered
Ownership: Nonprofit
Residency requirement: No residency required

Tuition:
$3,000 to $5,000 depending on which payment plan is used

Fields of study or special interest:
Taxation (M.Tax. for accountants, LL.M. for lawyers)

Other information:
A graduate-level educational program covering the American law of taxation. It consists of thirty semester units (four hundred hours of instruction). A portion of the requirements may be satisfied by transfer credits, independent research, or a thesis. Most students take two years to complete the program.

The program is designed for lawyers, CPAs, and people with a Bachelor's in accounting, law, or a subject considered to be sufficiently preparatory for graduate-level tax studies (finance, banking, economics, etc.).

Students take one course at a time using what the school calls the most advanced integrated system of textbooks on taxation of any graduate tax program. Lectures are available on video cassette. Students also have required assignments and tests (open book).

Students may engage in tax studies at a recognized professional education tax program and receive credit for up to fifteen semester units (in place of certain classes) but this must be done while enrolled in Washington School of Law (no credit given for studies taken before enrollment).

The doctorate (J.S.D. for lawyers, Ph.D. for CPAs) requires the Master's in taxation, and a book-length dissertation of publishable quality, which must be defended before a specialist panel.

The school is accepted for CPE credit by the Treasury, Internal Revenue Service for Enrolled Agents, and by the state boards of accountancy of virtually all states requiring such approval. The college is registered with the Utah Board of Regents. It is a division of Washington Institute for Graduate Studies, a Utah educational corporation.

Accreditation from the unrecognized but legitimate National Association for Private Non--Traditional Schools and Colleges.

Western Illinois University

Accredited nonresident Bachelor's degree in many fields of study entirely through home study.

School of Continuing Education
Horrabin Hall 5
Macomb, IL 61455

Telephone: (309) 298-1929
Fax number: —

Toll-free phone: (800) 322-3902 (IL)
Year established: 1899

Degree levels available: Bachelor's
Key person: Dr. Hans Moll, Director, Non-Traditional Programs
Recognition: Accredited by North Central Association
Ownership: Nonprofit, state
Residency requirement: No residency required

Tuition:
The catalog reports that "total cost of the program depends on the number and type of courses taken and cost of assessing a life experience portfolio is only $30."

Fields of study or special interest:
Many fields; the program does not require a major (but you can have one if you want).

Other information:
Courses may be taken at the campus at Macomb, extension courses at locations around the state, or through the Independent Study Program (which means correspondence courses). Credit is given for a prior learning portfolio (experiential learning), and proficiency exams (CLEP and also proficiency exams are available for some courses) to create a personalized program of study.

Western Illinois provides a helpful guide to the preparation of a prior learning portfolio.

Fifteen units of a total of 120 must be at one or a combination of Board of Governors universities, but they can be done by correspondence.

Students who did not graduate from an Illinois high school must pass an exam on the U.S. and Illinois state constitutions, or take an equivalent course in political science. All students must pass a University Writing Exam.

Students from other countries are admitted, but they must have a U.S. address to which materials can be sent.

The university has "up-link" capabilities. They are working on being able to broadcast telecourses nationwide and are experimenting with BITNET communication between professors and students enrolled in various courses.

A similar program, but with some differences, is also offered by four other Board of Governors of State Colleges and Universities System. Chicago State University (95th Street at King Drive, Chicago, IL 60628), Eastern Illinois University (Charleston, IL 61920), Governors State University (University Park, IL 60466), and Northeastern Illinois University (5500 North St. Louis Avenue, Chicago, IL 60625).

Appendices

Appendix A

For More Information on Schools in This Book

IF YOU HAVE QUESTIONS about one of the hundred schools described in this book, don't hesitate to write to me. I'll do my best to help. These are the ground rules:

What to do before writing to me

◆ Do your homework. Check with your local library or the relevant state education department or the Better Business Bureau before writing to me.
◆ Schools do move, and the Post Office will only forward mail for a short while. If a letter comes back as "undeliverable," then call Directory Assistance ("Information") in their city and see if they have a phone.
◆ Schools do change their phone numbers, and the telephone companies will only notify you of the new number for a short while. If you can't reach a school by phone, write them or try Information in their city to see if there has been a change.

Writing to me

◆ If you cannot reach them by phone or mail . . . or if you have new information you think I should know . . . or if you have questions or problems, then please write to let me know. I may be able to help.
◆ Enclose a self-addressed stamped envelope. If you are outside the U.S., enclose two International Postal Reply Coupons, available at your post office.
◆ If you want extensive advice or opinions on your personal situation, you will need to use the Degree Consulting Service which I established (although I no longer run it), which is described in Appendix C.
◆ Don't get too annoyed if I don't respond promptly. I do my best, but I get overwhelmed sometimes, and I travel a lot.
◆ Please don't telephone.
◆ Write to me thus:

> Dr. John Bear,
> P.O. Box 1616-A
> Hilo, HI 96721 U.S.A.

Appendix B

For Information on Schools Not in This Book

THERE ARE TWO REASONS WHY a school in which you might be interested is not described in this book:

◆ It might have been relevant, but I chose not to make them one of the hundred described schools.

◆ It is not relevant for this book, since it does not offer degrees entirely or mostly by home study.

If you have questions about a school that is not described in this book, here is what I would suggest, in the following order:

1. Check Appendix D, where I have listed fifty schools that offer degrees by home study which are *not* described in this book. It might be there.

2. Look them up in one of the standard school directories which you should find in any public library or bookstore: Lovejoy's, Barron's, Peterson's, Patterson's, ARCO, Cass & Birnbaum, and half a dozen others. Those books describe virtually every traditional college and university in the U.S. and Canada.

3. Ask for the help of a reference librarian. Your tax dollars pay their salaries.

4. If you know the location of the school, even the state, check with the relevant state education agency.

5. See if they are listed in another book I have written, which has shorter listings for hundreds more nontraditional schools in the U.S. and other countries. This book is called *Bear's Guide to Earning College Degrees Non-Traditionally,* published by the Greenwich University Press, and available only by mail from F. & K. Costedoat, Box 826-T, Benicia, CA 94510. Ask for a free sixteen-page descriptive booklet. To know whether my other book includes information on any given school, the school index to that book is reproduced, in absurdly small type, in Appendix I of this book.

If none of the above approaches produce any useful information, then write to me and I will do what I can to help.

◆ Enclose a self-addressed stamped envelope.

◆ If you want extensive advice or opinions on your personal situation, you will need to use the Degree Consulting Service which I established (although I no longer run it), which is described in Appendix C.

◆ Don't get too annoyed if I don't respond promptly. I do my best, but I get overwhelmed sometimes, and I travel a lot.

◆ Please don't telephone.

◆ Write to me thus:

Dr. John Bear
P.O. Box 1616-A
Hilo, HI 96721 USA

Appendix C

For Personal Advice on Your Own Situation

IF YOU WOULD LIKE personal advice and recommendations, based on your own specific situation, a personal counseling service is available, by mail. I started this service in 1977, at the request of many readers. The actual personal evaluations and consulting are done by two friends and colleagues of mine, who are leading experts in the field of nontraditional education.

For the modest consulting fee of $50, these things are done:

1. You will get a long personal letter (usually four to six typewritten pages) evaluating your situation, recommending the best degree programs for you (including part-time programs in your area) and estimating how long it will take and what it will cost you to complete your degree(s).

2. You will get answers to any specific questions you may have, with regard to any programs you may now be considering, institutions you have already dealt with, or other relevant matters.

3. You will get detailed, up-to-the-minute information on institutions and degree programs, equivalency exams, sources of the correspondence courses you may need, career opportunities, resumé writing, sources of financial aid, and other topics, in the form of prepared notes (some thirty pages of these) and a large sixteen-page booklet.

4. You will be able to telephone or write the service, to get as much follow-up counseling as you want, to keep updated on new programs and other changes, and to use the service as your personal information resource.

If you are interested in this personal counseling, please write or call and you will be sent descriptive literature and a counseling questionnaire, without cost or obligation.

Once you have these materials, if you wish counseling, simply fill out the questionnaire and return it, with a letter and resume if you like, along with the fee, and your personal reply and counseling materials will be airmailed to you.

For free information, write or telephone:

Degree Consulting Services
P. O. Box 3533
Santa Rosa, California 95402
(707) 539-6466

NOTE: Use this address only to reach the counseling service. For all other matters, please write to me at P.O. Box 1616-A, Hilo, HI 96721. Thank you.

Appendix D
Fifty Schools that Are Not in This Book

THERE ARE MORE THAN 5,000 degree-granting colleges and universities on this planet, which means that more than 4,900 have not been included in this book: most because they do not offer relevant degree programs; some because they are terrible places that you don't want to deal with, and some because there just wasn't room for everyone and some schools had to be left out.

Here are brief descriptions of fifty degree-granting institutions that were not included, along with my reasons for exclusion. I am putting these in because they are schools I am often asked about. Some are excellent, some are terrible, some are in between.

AMERICAN HOLISTIC COLLEGE OF NUTRITION, Alabama
See Chadwick University.

AMERICAN INSTITUTE OF COMPUTER SCIENCES, Alabama
See Chadwick University.

AMERICAN INTERNATIONAL UNIVERSITY, California
Diploma mill established by Edward Reddeck, later to move on to the currently flourishing phony University of North America.

AMERICAN NATIONAL UNIVERSITY, California
Major diploma mill that operated worldwide in the 70's and 80's.

ANDREW JACKSON UNIVERSITY or COLLEGE, Maryland
Unaccredited school established in Louisiana by Dr. Jean-Maximillien De La Croix de Lafayette, lawyer, author, and art patron; later moved to Maryland; now apparently dormant.

ANGLO-AMERICAN INSTITUTE OF DRUGLESS THERAPY, Scotland
Unaccredited nonresident Doctorates in naturopathy.

BARD COLLEGE, New York
A short-residency Bachelor's degree designed "to meet the special needs of adults who have left college . . ." Students meet with tutors twice a month.

BEREAN COLLEGE, Missouri
Accredited nonresident Bachelor's degrees in religious subjects.

BERNADEAN UNIVERSITY, California
Correspondence law and other degrees. For a time, offered a certificate good for absolution of all sins with each degree.

BETA INTERNATIONAL UNIVERSITY, Missouri
Unaccredited school of the Brotherhood of Beta Phi Epsilon, offering degrees at all levels by correspondence. Only name in the catalog is "Dr. Ellis."

CALIFORNIA PACIFICA UNIVERSITY, California
Major diploma mill exposed by *60 Minutes* in 1978; the proprietor went to prison.

CALIFORNIA UNIVERSITY FOR ADVANCED STUDIES, California
One of California's larger nonresident universities, lost their license to operate and went out of business in 1990.

CHADWICK UNIVERSITY, Alabama
Dr. Lloyd Clayton operates four institutions of higher learning from the same address. They have nearly identical small catalogs that do not mention faculty or staff. The programs are all inexpensive and not excessively arduous. Dr. Clayton has been invited to stop accepting students by the state of Alabama, but this does not affect his out-of-state operations.

CLAYTON UNIVERSITY, Missouri
In previous books, I have said good and positive things about Clayton. However, my mail to their street address was returned as undeliverable, and my mail to the P.O. box to which their letters were being forwarded has never been answered.

COLORADO STATE UNIVERSITY, Colorado
Their SURGE program, in the Division of Continuing Education, does lots of interesting things at the Master's level, but they don't want to be in this book.

COLUMBIA STATE UNIVERSITY, Louisiana
The address is a mail forwarding service which reported that they send the mail to California.

COLUMBIA UNIVERSITY, New York
They have an innovative Doctor of Education program called AEGIS (Adult Education Guided Independent Study), which can be earned by attending seminars one weekend day a month for two years plus a three-week summer intensive.

CORNERSTONE THEOLOGICAL SEMINARY, Texas
Nonresident degrees of all kinds. They claim (incorrectly) to be accredited by the State of Israel, by Washington, and by Louisiana.

DARTMOUTH COLLEGE, New Hampshire
They have an M.A. in liberal studies which can be earned by attending for three consecutive summers.

DYKE COLLEGE, Ohio
Very short residency Bachelor's degrees for people living in or near Cleveland.

EULA WESLEY UNIVERSITY, Louisiana

They are really in Arizona, where the Phoenix newspaper reports that the founder, Dr. Samuel Wesley, runs things from his home. Dr. Wesley's Doctorate is from Eula Wesley University.

EVERYMAN'S UNIVERSITY, Israel

An excellent nonresident university, but the work must be done in Hebrew.

FAIRFAX UNIVERSITY, Louisiana

An academically sound program, although the premises are a secretarial service which forwards mail and messages to England. The only complaints I have gotten have been regarding the difficulty of reaching people. (The University announced, for instance, that it would close down entirely, no mail or phone calls or visits, for two of the last five months of 1990.) My wife and I were two of the four founders, but we resigned about two months after the first students enrolled in 1986. Although I thought we had parted company amicably, within weeks President Jones was attempting (unsuccessfully) to get authorities in California to enjoin me from selling my book on degrees, because he did not like certain things I said in it.

FERNUNIVERSITÄT, Germany

An excellent nonresident university in Germany which, not surprisingly, requires all work to be done in German.

FLAMING RAINBOW UNIVERSITY, Oklahoma

One of my favorite school names; short-residency Bachelor's degrees, primarily for Native Americans.

HARVARD UNIVERSITY, Massachusetts

You can actually do half of a Harvard Bachelor's degree by correspondence, then spend two years there and get a Bachelor of Liberal Arts.

INDIANA UNIVERSITY OF PENNSYLVANIA, Pennsylvania

Ph.D. in literature which can be earned at two summer sessions.

INTERNATIONAL INSTITUTE FOR ADVANCED STUDIES, Missouri

Dormant at this time; the degree programs are now part of Greenwich University, which is described in this book.

INTERNATIONAL UNIVERSITY, Missouri

Claims offices all over the world; claims accreditation from an unrecognized agency; no faculty listed in catalog.

INTERNATIONAL UNIVERSITY, New York

They claim to operate from the island of St. Kitts, but apparently actually do so from New York. They have never responded to my many letters.

INTERNATIONAL UNIVERSITY FOR NUTRITION EDUCATION, California

Formerly Donsbach University, offering nonresident degrees in nutritional areas.

KENT COLLEGE, Louisiana

The address is the Church of Jesus of the Eternal Light. President Delmer Robinson, formerly with Fairfax University, apparently lives in Florida.

LA SALLE UNIVERSITY, Louisiana
The address is a small rural church, but the scope of the operation belies this setting. There are at least half a dozen toll-free numbers. Accreditation is claimed from an unrecognized organization established by the people who run La Salle, and who previously ran the now defunct Southland University in California.

LONDON SCHOOL FOR SOCIAL RESEARCH, London
Nonexistent school that resurfaces from time to time, selling fake degrees.

LOUISIANA PACIFIC UNIVERSITY, Louisiana
The address is a secretarial service.

METROPOLITAN STATE UNIVERSITY, Minnesota
Very short residency degrees, primarily for Minnesotans.

NORTH AMERICAN UNIVERSITY, Utah and perhaps elsewhere
A notorious diploma mill, run by Edward Reddeck, who had previously served time in prison for educational scams. This one was started in Missouri, where it was shut down by the Attorney General and fined $2,500,000. He fled to Utah, where at press time he was still operating, despite the efforts of various authorities to close him down once again.

NOVA COLLEGE, Canada and perhaps elsewhere
No new work is required to earn Nova's degrees. Nova has complained about things I have said about them in the past. I tried to call to discuss their concerns, but they apparently had no telephone. No connection with Nova University of Florida.

OPEN UNIVERSITY OF THE NETHERLANDS
Holland's nonresident university. All work must be done in Dutch.

PACIFIC COAST UNIVERSITY, New York and Louisiana
The addresses are secretarial services.

REID COLLEGE OF DETECTION OF DECEPTION, Illinois
Unaccredited Master's in polygraph use, based on a six-month course.

SAINT JOHN'S UNIVERSITY, Louisiana
Run from the President's home, they offer a wide range of degrees by correspondence, and do not ask too much of their students.

SOMERSET UNIVERSITY, Louisiana and England
Although they have received a lot of bad press in England, what they are doing is clearly legal, and a considerable improvement over President Raymond Young's previous ventures, the almost nonexistent Harley University and St. Giles University College.

SOUTHWESTERN UNIVERSITY, Arizona
Major diploma mill operating in the 80's; the proprietor was sent to prison.

SUSSEX COLLEGE OF TECHNOLOGY, England

A well-known British degree mill which advertises extensively in the U.S. and elsewhere. Some people do some work for the degrees, but others just pay the fee for whatever they want. When the law required them to stop offering degrees to people who applied after a certain date, they simply began back-dating the applications, and roll merrily along.

THEOLOGICAL UNIVERSITY OF AMERICA, Louisiana

See University of America.

UNIVERSAL LIFE UNIVERSITY, California

Run by the Universal Life Church; an offering of up to $100 gets you the degree of your choice.

UNIVERSITY DE LA ROMANDE, England

A non-wonderful English school that once claimed to be a fully accredited Swiss school.

UNIVERSITY OF AMERICA, Louisiana

The same management as the Theological University of America; the catalogs are identical but for a few religious references in the latter. The listed faculty have good credentials (but for the president, who declines to identify the source of his Doctorate). The address is a mail forwarding service.

UNIVERSITY OF BEVERLY HILLS, Iowa

They tell authorities they are no longer operating, but they continue to advertise in Spain, Malaysia, and elsewhere.

UNIVERSITY OF EAST GEORGIA, Georgia

Phony school whose owner was nabbed by the FBI and sent to prison.

UNIVERSITY OF ENGLAND, Oxford

Nonexistent but heavily advertised school; I had the pleasure of testifying against their founders, five of whom went to prison in 1989.

UNIVERSITY OF NORTH AMERICA, Missouri

The former name of the diploma mill now called North American University. They advertised widely in *USA Today* and other national publications and sold degrees to a great many people, some of them willing coconspirators and some actually believing they had earned the degree from a reputable school.

UNIVERSITY OF PHOENIX, Arizona

Their well-regarded M.B.A. can be earned "on line" over a home computer network.

UNIVERSITY OF SANTA MONICA, California

Unaccredited but reputable school, formerly Koh-E-Nor University.

WEBSTER UNIVERSITY, Missouri

They offer innovative and well-regarded Master's programs, but their Coordinator of Experiential and Individual Learning wrote to demand that I stop providing information on them, which I am happy to do. It must be very satisfying to have all the students one could ever want.

WESTERN STATES UNIVERSITY
They operate legally in Missouri, offering nonresident degrees, but their founder has two phony degrees of his own.

WILLIAM LYON UNIVERSITY, California
Unaccredited but state-approved degrees at all levels, with no visits to campus, but in-person meetings with faculty mentors.

WORLD UNIVERSITY OF AMERICA, California
Unaccredited, but state approved, with opportunity to earn degrees in astrology, out of body experience, avasthology, and spiritual ministry.

☛ *Last Minute Update!*

GOLD COAST UNIVERSITY, Hawaii
In 1991, Edward Reddeck, proprietor of North American University (see next page), and several other fake schools, established yet another diploma mill, from a mail forwarding and telephone answering service in Hawaii.

Appendix E

The Situation in California

AT ONE TIME, CALIFORNIA had more unaccredited colleges and universities than the other forty-nine states combined: over two hundred in the 1970s. But in 1989, a series of laws were passed and signed by the governor which changed drastically the way California will handle the matter of school licensing, particularly with regard to unaccredited schools. The number of unaccredited schools has plummeted. Some moved to other states; some merged with other schools; some went out of business; some are openly or secretly for sale; and more than a few have plans they have not yet revealed.

The problem right now (Spring, 1991) is that it is very unclear how things will shake down in that state. Not only are new guidelines still being developed and new committees and commissions being appointed, but more than a few schools have announced that they are going to challenge the new regulations in court.

It may be years before the situation in California is fully resolved and clear.

The one thing that *is* clear is that matters are now in the hands of a new state agency: the Council for Private Postsecondary and Vocational Education, located at 1020 12th Street, Sacramento, CA 95814, (916) 445-3427.

What may happen in California: the strict interpretation

Three senior staff members of the new commission published a "position paper" advocating strict interpretation of the new laws. If they have their way, the following things will happen, among others:

- ◆ State authorized schools will no longer be allowed to operate; only state approved schools will be permitted.
- ◆ State approved schools will no longer be able to offer Doctorates by correspondence or external study.
- ◆ State approved schools would have a certain period of time to become a candidate for accreditation or they could no longer operate (the so-called "up or out" provision).
- ◆ No school can offer degrees in psychology by correspondence study.
- ◆ The amount of credit given for prior learning would be severely restricted.
- ◆ Schools offering vocational training would have to prove that a high percentage of their graduates are employed in the field of study after graduation.
- ◆ Out-of-state law schools can no longer offer correspondence study for the California Bar exam.

What may happen in California: the lenient interpretation

Three presidents of unaccredited California schools who serve on the new commission, and others, believe the staff recommendations just mentioned are far too severe, and they do not think those recommendations should be accepted. They acknowledge that the category of "state authorized" schools must go, but they believe that state approved schools should be permitted to operate in a manner much as they do now, including offering Doctorates, degrees in psychology, etc.

As I write these words in the spring of 1991, it is a time of uncertainty in California. Several large schools have closed down, and others are rumored to be in severe financial trouble. A dozen or more have moved to other states: Louisiana, Iowa, New Mexico, Idaho, and Hawaii. The rest undoubtedly have contingency plans, and are awaiting further developments. By the time you read this, things may have all been resolved, one way or the other.

Bear in mind that California schools listed in this book will be no less good (or bad, as the case may be) even if they move to another state. But before you choose a California school, you may wish to call or write the new Council in Sacramento for an update, or to ask the schools themselves what their plans are as a result of the new laws. Will they be moving, merging, changing their method of operation, or closing down? You must consider how this situation might affect you, if you choose to be a student.

Appendix F
Bending the Rules

ONE OF THE MOST COMMON COMPLAINTS or admonishments I get from readers takes the form of "You said thus-and-so, but when I inquired of the school, they told me such-and-such." Often, a school claims that a program I have written about does not exist. Sometimes a student achieves something (such as completing a certain degree entirely by correspondence) that I had been told by a high official of the school was impossible.

One of the open "secrets" in the world of higher education is that the rules are constantly being bent. But, like the Emperor's new clothes, no one dares point and say what is really going on, especially in print.

The purpose of this brief essay is to acknowledge that this sort of thing happens all the time. If you know that it happens regularly, then at least you are in the same boat with people who are benefiting already by virtue of bent rules.

Unfortunately, I cannot provide many specific examples of bent rules, naming names and all. This is for two good reasons:

1. Many situations where students profit from bent rules would disappear in an instant if anyone dared mention the situation publicly. There is, for instance, a major state university that is forbidden by its charter from granting degrees for correspondence study. But they regularly work out special arrangements for students, who are carried on the books as residential students, even though all work is done by mail, and some of the graduates have never set foot on the campus. If this ever "got out," the Board of Trustees, the accrediting agency, and all the other universities in that state would probably have conniptions, and the practice would be suspended at once.

2. These kinds of things can change so rapidly, with new personnel or new policies, that a listing of anomalies and curious practices would probably be obsolete before the ink dried.

Consider a few examples of the sort of thing that is going on in higher education every day, whether or not anyone will admit it, except perhaps behind closed doors or after several drinks:

◆ A friend of mine, at a major university, was unable to complete one required course for her Doctorate, before she had to leave for another state. This university does not offer correspondence courses, but she was able to convince a professor to enroll her in a regular course, which she would just "happen" never to visit in person.

◆ A man in graduate school needed to be enrolled in nine units of coursework each semester to keep his employer's tuition assistance plan going. But his job was too demanding one year, and he was unable to do so. The school enrolled him in nine units of "independent study" for which no work was asked or required, and for which a "pass" grade was given.

◆ A woman at a large school needed to get a certain number of units before an inflexible time deadline. When it was clear she was not going to make it, a kindly professor turned in grades for her, and told her she could do the actual coursework later on.

◆ A major state university offers nonresident degrees for people living in that state only. When a reader wrote me to say that he, living a thousand miles from that state, was able to complete his degree entirely by correspondence, I asked a contact at that school what was going on. "We will take students from anywhere in our correspondence degree program," she told me, "But for God's sake, don't print that in your book, or we'll be deluged with applicants."

◆ If we are to believe a book by a member of Dr. Bill Cosby's dissertation committee at the University of Massachusetts (*Education's Smoking Gun* by Reginald Damerell), the only class attendance on Cosby's transcript was one weekend seminar, and the only dissertation committee meeting was a dinner party, with spouses, at Cosby's house.

◆ Part way through my final doctoral oral exam, a key member of my committee had to leave for an emergency. He scrawled a note, and passed it to the Dean who read it, then crumpled it up and threw it away. The grueling exam continued for several hours more. After it was over and the committee had congratulated me and departed, I retrieved the note from the wastebasket. It read, "Please give John my apologies for having to leave, and my congratulations for having passed."

◆ A man applied to a well-known school that has a rigid requirement that all graduate work (thesis or dissertation) must be begun after enrollment. He started to tell an admissions officer about a major piece of independent research he had completed for his employer. "Stop," he was told, "Don't tell me about that. Then you will be able to use it for your Master's thesis."

◆ My eldest daughter was denied admission to the University of California at Berkeley because of some "irregularities" on her high school transcript. (It was a nontraditional high school.) The high school's records had been destroyed in a fire. The former principal checked with the University, discovered that the admissions people would be glad to admit her, once the computer said it was okay. He typed up a new transcript saying what the computer wanted said. The computer said okay, and three years later, said daughter graduated Phi Beta Kappa. But how many other applicants accepted the initial "No," not knowing that rules can often be bent?

Please use this information prudently. It will probably do no good to pound on a table and say, "What do you mean I can't do this? John Bear says that rules don't mean anything, anyway."

But when faced with a problem, it surely can do no harm to remember that there do exist many situations in which the rules have turned out to be far less rigid than the printed literature of a school would lead one to believe.

Appendix G
Advice for People in Prison

NOTE: More than a few readers and users of this book are people who are institutionalized, or friends and relatives of those who are. For this edition, I have invited a man who has completed his Bachelor's and Master's from prison, and who consults often with inmates and others around the country, to offer his thoughts and recommendations. There is some very useful advice for noninstitutionalized persons as well.

Arranging Academic Resources for the Institutionalized

by Douglas G. Dean

One obstacle for any institutionalized person interested in pursuing a degree is limited resources: availability of community faculty, library facilities, phone access, and financial aid. To overcome these, it helps to streamline the matriculation process. Time spent in preparation prior to admission can help avoid wasted effort and time when in a program, thereby reducing operating expenses and cutting down the number of tuition periods.

A second obstacle is finding ways to ensure that a quality education can be documented. Because courses are generally not prepackaged, it is the student's responsibility to identify varied learning settings, use varied learning methods, find and recruit community-based faculty, provide objective means to appraise what has been learned, and indeed design the study plan itself.

Find a flexible degree program

Most well-established degree programs grant credit for a variety of learning experiences. In terms of cost and arrangements required, equivalency examinations and independent study projects are the most expedient. Credit for life experience learning is another option sometimes offered. If a degree program does not offer at least these first two options, it is unlikely that the program as a whole will be able to accommodate the needs of the institutionalized student.

Write a competency-based study plan

The traditional method of acquiring credits is to take narrowly focused courses of two to four credits each. Since the nontraditional student must enlist his or her own instructors, find varied learning methods, and quantify the whole experience, the single course approach creates much needless duplication of effort.

A better approach is to envision a subject area which is to be studied for nine to twelve credits (e.g., statistics). As an independent study project, the student identifies what topics are germane to the area (e.g., probability theory, descriptive statistics, inferential statistics); at what level of comprehension (e.g., introductory through intermediate or advanced); how the topic is to be studied (e.g., directed reading, programmed textbooks), and how the competencies acquired are to be demonstrated (e.g., oral examination, proctored examination including problem solving). This way, a single independent study project can take the place of a series of successive courses in a given area (e.g., statistics 101, 201, 301).

Designing the curriculum

Every accredited degree program has graduation requirements. These requirements broadly define the breadth of subject areas that comprise a liberal arts education and the depth to which they are to be studied. It is the responsibility of the external student not only to identify a curriculum fulfilling these requirements, but in most cases to design the course content that will comprise each study module.

But how does a student know what an area of study consists of before he or she has studied it? The answer lies in meticulous preparation.

Well in advance of formally applying for an off-campus degree program, the prospective student should obtain course catalogs from several colleges and universities. Look at what these schools consider the core curriculum, and what is necessary to fulfill the graduation requirements. With the broad outline in mind, the student can begin to form clusters of courses fulfilling each criterion. This helps shape the study plan academically rather than touch it up later as an afterthought.

Next, decide which subjects are of interest within each criterion area. Compare topical areas within each subject as described in the course listings, and commonalities will emerge. From there, it is simply a matter of writing to the various instructors for copies of their course syllabuses. These course outlines will provide more detailed information about the subject matter and identify the textbooks currently used at that level of study.

Means of study

Having decided what is to be studied, the student must then propose various ways to study it.

Equivalency exams enable the student to acquire credits instantly, often in core or required areas of study. This helps reduce overall program costs by eliminating the need for textbooks and tuition fees. More importantly, it helps reduce the number of special learning arrangements that must otherwise be made.

"Testing out" of correspondence courses (taking only the examinations, without doing the homework assignments) is another excellent way to acquire credits quickly. This can, however, be an expensive method since full course fees are still assessed. Nonetheless, if a student studies on his or her own in advance according to the course syllabus, and if the instructor can then be convinced to waive prerequisite assignments, it can be an efficient and cost-effective method to use.

Independent study projects should form the balance of any study plan. With the topical areas, learning objectives, and learning materials identified, an independent study project allows the student to remain with the same instructor(s) from an introductory through an intermediate or advanced level of study. This eliminates the need for new arrangements to be made every two to four credits. An independent study project can take the form of simple directed reading, tutorial instruction, practicum work, or a combination of these methods, culminating in the final product.

Independent study projects require the aid of qualified persons to act as community faculty, and to oversee personally the progress of the work. Therefore it is highly advantageous to line up faculty in advance of entering the degree program, and to have alternates available in the event an instructor is unable, for any reason, to fulfill his or her commitment. It is better to anticipate these needs at the preparatory stage than to be scrambling for a replacement while the tuition clock is running.

Multiple treatments of subject matter

The external student is without benefit of lecture halls, interactions with other students, or readily available academic counseling services. For the institutionalized student, picking up the phone or stopping in to see a faculty member for help with a study problem is not an option. This is why alternate methods of study are so valuable.

One approach is to use several textbooks covering the same subject matter. If something does not make sense, there is a different treatment of the subject to turn to.

Programmed textbooks make especially good substitute tutors. A programmed text breaks the subject matter into small segments requiring a response from the reader with periodic tests to check progress. Such texts are now available in many subject areas, but are particularly useful for the sciences. Titles can be learned from the subject guide to *Books in Print,* or by writing directly to textbook publishers.

Audio-visual materials can, to some extent, make up for college life without lectures and classes. Writing to A-V (audio-visual) departments at large universities often yields a catalog of materials available for rental. When using such materials, it is best to work through the school or social service department of the student's institution of residence.

Some large campuses have lecture note services, in which advanced students attend introductory lectures, and take copious lecture notes, which are then sold to students. Aside from their insights into good note-taking, these published notes are an additional treatment of course content. Such notes are especially recommended for new students.

Documenting study

The administrators of a degree program must be convinced that there are acceptable ways to document what has been learned, and what levels of subject mastery have been achieved, without taking the student's word for it. Community faculty members may be asked to provide written or oral examinations, but it does not hurt to make their jobs easier.

Most professions (accounting, psychology, law, medicine, etc.) have licensing and/or board certification examinations that must be taken. An industry has built up around this need, providing parallel or actual past examinations to help prepare students. By agreeing to take a relevant sample examination under proctored conditions, and negotiating a "pass" score in advance, the community faculty member is relieved of having to design his or her own objective examination for just one student. This approach adds validity to the assessment process, and provides a standardized score that has some universal meaning. This is an optional approach but may be worth the effort.

Recruiting community faculty

Just as it is easier for a student to organize a study plan in blocks of subject areas, a competency-based study plan of this sort makes it easier for a prospective instructor to visualize what is being asked of him or her.

A typical independent study project would define for the instructor what specific topics are to be studied, what levels of mastery will be expected of the student, what textbooks or other materials will be used, and what is expected of the instructor.

Many traditional academics are unfamiliar with external degree programs. Consequently, they tend to assume that their role as instructor will require greater effort and time on their part than for the average student, who may expect their services in many roles, from academic advisor to tutor. The more an institutionalized student can do up front to define clearly the role and expected duties of the community faculty member, the more successful a student will be in enlisting instructors for independent study projects.

Instructors may sometimes be found on the staff of the institution where the student resides. They may also be found through a canvas letter sent to the appropriate department heads at area colleges, universities, and technical schools. The same approach may be used to canvas departments within area businesses, museums, art centers, hospitals, libraries, theaters, zoos, banks, and orchestras, to name but a few. People are often flattered to be asked, providing it is clear to them exactly what they are getting into.

The more a student can operate independently, and rely on community faculty for little more than assessment purposes, the more likely a student will be successful in recruiting help, and thereby broadening the range of study options.

"Revealing" your institutionalized status

It is generally proper and appropriate to inform potential schools and potential faculty of one's institutionalized status. (Many institutions now have mailing addresses that do not indicate they are, in fact, institutions.) Some schools or individuals may be "put off" by this, but then you would not want to deal with them anyway. Others may be especially motivated to help.

Financing the educational process

Unfortunately, there are virtually no generalizations to be made here, whatsoever. Each institution seems to have its own policy with regard to the way finances are handled. Some institutionalized persons earn decent wages, and have access to the funds. Others have little or no ability to pay their own way. Some institutions permit financial gifts from relatives or friends, others do not. Some schools make special concessions or have some scholarship funds available for institutionalized persons; many do not. One should contact the financial aid office of the school to ask this question.

Some people have had success in approaching foundations for this purpose. One foundation that has specialized in helping incarcerated people pursue accredited degrees is the Davis-Putter Fund, 1820 Fleming Road, Louisville, KY 40205.

At the Bachelor's level, Ohio University offers degrees by correspondence study especially for people in prison, at significantly lower tuition than their usual programs.

In conclusion

Institutionalized students must be highly self-directed, and honest enough with themselves to recognize if they are not. Because the student lives where he or she works, it takes extra effort to set aside daily study time, not only to put the student in the right frame of mind, but also to accommodate institution schedules. It can mean working with a minimum number of books or tapes to comply with property rules. It means long periods of delayed gratification, in an environment where pursuing education is often suspect. And it is the greatest feeling in the world when it all comes together.

Appendix H
Glossary of Important Terms

academic year: The period of formal academic instruction, usually from September or October to May or June, divided into semesters, quarters, or trimesters.

accreditation: Recognition of a school by an independent private organization. Not a governmental function in the U.S. There are more than one hundred accrediting agencies, some recognized by the Department of Education and/or COPA, and some unrecognized, some phony or fraudulent.

ACT: American College Testing program, administrators of aptitude and achievement tests.

adjunct faculty: Part-time faculty member, often at a nontraditional school, often with a full-time teaching job elsewhere. More and more traditional schools are hiring adjunct faculty, because they don't have to pay them as much or provide health care and other benefits.

advanced placement: Admission to a school at a higher level than one would normally enter at, because of getting credit for prior learning experience or passing advanced placement exams.

alma mater: The school from which one has graduated, as in "My alma mater is Michigan State University."

alternative: Used interchangeably with *external* or *nontraditional*; offering an alternate, or different means of pursuing learning or degrees or both.

alumni: Graduates of a school, as in "This school has some distinguished alumni." The word is technically for males only; females are *alumnae*. The singular is *alumnus* (male) or *alumna* (female).

alumni association: A confederation of alumni and alumnae who have joined together to support their alma mater in various ways, generally by donating money.

approved: In California, a level of state recognition of a school, generally regarded as one step above *authorized* and one step below *accredited.*

arbitration: A means of settling disputes, as between a student and a school, in which one or more independent arbitrators or judges listen to both sides, and make a decision. A means of avoiding a courtroom trial. Many learning contracts have an arbitration clause. (See *binding arbitration, mediation.*)

assistantship: A means of assisting students (usually graduate students) financially by offering them part-time academic employment, usually in the form of a teaching assistantship or a research assistantship.

Associate's degree: A "two-year" degree, traditionally awarded by community or junior colleges after two years of residential study, or completion of 60 to 64 semester hours.

auditing: Sitting in on a class without earning credit for that class.

authorized: In California, a form of state recognition of schools, authorizing them to exist, to accept students, and to grant degrees.

Bachelor's degree: Awarded in the U.S. after four years of full-time residential study (two to five years in other countries), or earning from 120 to 124 semester units by any means.

binding arbitration: Arbitration in which both parties have agreed in advance that they will abide by the result and take no further legal action.

branch campus: A satellite facility, run by officers of the main campus of a college or university, at another location. Can range from a small office to a full-fledged university center.

campus: The main facility of a college or university, usually comprising buildings, grounds, dormitories, cafeterias and dining halls, sports stadia, etc. The campus of a nontraditional school may consist solely of offices.

chancellor: Often the highest official of a university. Also a new degree title, proposed by some schools, to be a higher degree than the Doctorate, and requiring three to five years of additional study.

CLEP: The College-Level Examination Program, a series of equivalency examinations given nationally each month.

coeducational: Education of men and women on the same campus or in the same program. This is why female students are called coeds.

college: In the U.S., an institution offering programs leading to the Associate's, Bachelor's, and possibly higher degrees. Often used interchangeably with *university* although traditionally a university is a collection of colleges. In England and elsewhere, *college* may denote part of a university (Kings College, Cambridge) or a private high school (Eton College).

colloquium: A gathering of scholars to discuss a given topic over a period of a few hours to a few days. ("The university is sponsoring a colloquium on marine biology.")

community college: A two-year traditional school, offering programs leading to the Associate's degree and, typically, many noncredit courses in arts, crafts, and vocational fields for community members not interested in a degree. Also called *junior college*.

competency: The philosophy and practice of awarding credit or degrees based on learning skills, rather than time spent in courses.

COPA: The Council on Postsecondary Accreditation, a private nongovernmental organization that recognizes accrediting agencies.

correspondence course: A course offered by mail, completed entirely by home study, often with one or two proctored, or supervised examinations.

course: A specific unit of instruction, such as a course in microeconomics, or a course in abnormal psychology. Residential courses last for one or more semesters or quarters; correspondence courses often have no rigid time requirements.

cramming: Intensive preparation for an examination. Most testing agencies now admit that cramming can improve scores on exams.

credit: Units used to record courses taken. Each credit typically represents the number of hours spent in class each week. Hence a three-credit or three-unit course would commonly be a class that met three hours each week for one semester or quarter.

curriculum: A program of courses to be taken in pursuit of a degree or other objective.

degree: A title conferred by a school to show that a certain course of study has been completed.

Department of Education: In the U.S., the national agency concerned with all educational matters not handled by the Departments of Education in the fifty states. In other countries, commonly the Ministry of Education.

diploma: The certificate that shows that a certain course of study has been completed. Diplomas are awarded for completing degree studies or other, shorter courses of study.

dissertation: The major research project normally required as part of the work for a Doctorate. Dissertations are expected to make a new and creative contribution to the field of study, or to demonstrate one's excellence in the field. (See also *thesis*.)

Doctorate: The highest degree one can earn (but see *chancellor*). Includes Doctor of Philosophy, Education, and many other titles.

dormitory: Student living quarters on residential campuses. May include dining halls and classrooms.

early decision: Making a decision on whether to admit a student sooner than decisions are usually made. Offered by some schools primarily as a service either to students applying to several schools, or those who are especially anxious to know the outcome of their application.

ECFMG: The Education Commission for Foreign Medical Graduates, which administers an examination to physicians who have gone to medical school outside the U.S. and wish to practice in the U.S.

electives: Courses one does not have to take, but may elect to take as part of a degree program.

essay test: An examination in which the student writes narrative sentences as answers to questions, instead of the short answers required by a multiple-choice test. Also called a *subjective test*.

equivalency examination: An examination designed to demonstrate knowledge in a subject where the learning was acquired outside a traditional classroom. A person who learned certain nursing skills while working in a hospital, for instance, could take an equivalency exam to earn credit in obstetrical nursing.

external: Away from the main campus or offices. An external degree may be earned by home study or at locations other than on the school's campus.

fees: Money paid to a school for purposes other than academic tuition. Fees might pay for parking, library services, use of the gymnasium, binding of dissertations, etc.

fellowship: A study grant, usually awarded to a graduate student, and usually requiring no work other than usual academic work (as contrasted with an *assistantship*).

financial aid: A catchall term, including scholarships, loans, fellowships, assistantships, tuition reductions, etc. Many schools have a financial aid officer.

fraternities: Men's fraternal and social organizations, often identified by Greek letters, such as Zeta Beta Tau. There are also professional and scholastic fraternities open to men and women, such as Beta Alpha Psi, the national fraternity for students of accounting.

freshman: The name for the class in its first of four years of traditional study for a Bachelor's degree, and its individual members. ("She is a freshman, and so is in the freshman class.")

glossary: What you are reading now. But is anyone reading it? To help me know this, I will send a dramatic volcano eruption postcard to anyone who writes to tell me they have seen this notice. John Bear, Box 1616-A, Hilo, Hawaii 96721, U.S.A.

grade point average: The average score a student has made in all his or her classes, weighted by the number of credits or units for each class. Also called G.P.A.

grades: Evaluative scores provided for each course, and often for individual examinations or papers written for that course. There are letter grades (usually A, B, C, D, F) and number grades (usually percentages from 0% to 100%), or on a scale of 0 to 3, 0 to 4, or 0 to 5. Some schools use a pass/fail system with no grades.

graduate: One who has earned a degree from a school, or the programs offered beyond the Bachelor's level. ("He is a graduate of Yale University, and is now working on his Master's in graduate school at Princeton.")

graduate school: A school or a division of a university offering work at the Master's or Doctoral degree level.

graduate student: One attending graduate school.

GRE: The Graduate Record Examination, which many traditional schools and a few nontraditional ones require for admission to graduate programs.

honor societies: Organizations for persons with a high grade point average or other evidence of outstanding performance. There are local societies on some campuses, and several national organizations, the most prestigious of which is called Phi Beta Kappa.

honor system: A system in which students are trusted not to cheat on examinations, and to obey other rules, without proctors or others monitoring their behavior.

honorary doctorate: A nonacademic award, given regularly by more than one thousand colleges and universities to honor distinguished scholars, celebrities, and donors of large sums of money. Holders of this award may, and often do, call themselves "Doctor."

junior: The name for the class in its third year of a traditional four-year U.S. Bachelor's degree program, or any member of that class. ("She is a junior this year, and is organizing the junior class prom.")

junior college: Same as *community college.*

language laboratory: A room with special audio equipment to facilitate learning languages by listening to tapes. Many students can be learning different languages at different skill levels at the same time.

learning contract: A formal agreement between a student and a school, specifying independent work to be done by the student, and the amount of credit the school will award on successful completion of the work.

lecture class: A course in which a faculty member lectures to anywhere from a few dozen to many hundreds of students. Often lecture classes are followed by small group discussion sessions led by student assistants or junior faculty.

liberal arts: A term with many complex meanings, but generally referring to the nonscientific curriculum of a university: humanities, the arts, social sciences, history, and so forth.

liberal education: Commonly taken to be the opposite of a specialized education; one in which students are required to take courses in a wide range of fields, as well as courses in their major.

licensed: Holding a permit to operate. This can range from a difficult-to-obtain state school license to a simple local business license.

life experience portfolio: A comprehensive presentation listing and describing all learning experiences in a person's life, with appropriate documentation. The basic document used in assigning academic credit for life experience learning.

LSAT: The Law School Admission Test, required by most U.S. law schools of all applicants.

maintenance costs: The expenses incurred while attending school, other than tuition and fees. Includes room and board (food), clothing, laundry, postage, travel, etc.

major: The subject or academic department in which a student takes concentrated coursework, leading to a specialty. ("His major is in English literature; she is majoring in chemistry.")

mentor: Faculty member assigned to supervise independent study work at a nontraditional school; comparable to *adjunct faculty.*

minor: The secondary subject or academic department in which a student takes concentrated coursework. ("She has a major in art and a minor in biology.")

MSAT: The Medical School Admission Test, required by most U.S. medical schools of all applicants.

multiple-choice test: An examination in which the student chooses the best of several alternative answers provided for each question; also called an *objective test*. ("The capital city of England is (a) London, (b) Ostrogotz-Plakatz, (c) Tokyo, (d) none of the above.")

multiversity: A university system with two or more separate campuses, each a major university in its own right, such as the University of California or the University of Wisconsin.

narrative transcript: A transcript issued by a nontraditional school in which, instead of simply listing the courses completed and grades received, there is a narrative description of the work done and the school's rationale for awarding credit for that work.

nontraditional: Something done in other than the usual or traditional way. In education, refers to learning and degrees completed by methods other than spending many hours in classrooms and lecture halls.

nonresident: (1) A means of instruction in which the student does not need to visit the school; all work is done by correspondence, telephone, or exchange of audio tapes or videotapes; (2) A person who does not meet residency requirements of a given school and, as a result, often has to pay a higher tuition or fees.

objective test: An examination in which questions requiring a very short answer are posed. It can be multiple choice, true-false, fill-in-the-blank, etc. The questions are related to facts (thus objective) rather than to opinions (or subjective).

on the job: In the U.S., experience or training gained through employment, which may be converted to academic credit. In England, slang for "having sex," which either confuses or amuses English people who read about "credit for on-the-job experience."

open admissions: An admissions policy in which everyone who applies is admitted, on the theory that the ones who are unable to do university work will drop out before long.

out-of-state student: One from a state other than that in which the school is located. Because most state colleges and universities have much higher tuition rates for out-of-state students, many people attempt to establish legal residence in the same state as their school.

parallel instruction: A method in which nonresident students do exactly the same work as residential students, during the same general time periods, except they do it at home.

pass/fail option: Instead of getting a letter or number grade in a course, the student may elect, at the start of the course, a pass/fail option in which the only grades are either "pass" or "fail." Some schools permit students to elect this option on one or two of their courses each semester.

PEP: Proficiency Examination Program, a series of equivalency exams given nationally every few months.

plan of study: A detailed description of the program an applicant to a school plans to pursue. Many traditional schools ask for this as part of the admissions procedure. The plan of study should be designed to meet the objectives of the *statement of purpose*.

portfolio: See *life experience portfolio*.

prerequisites: Courses that must be taken before certain other courses may be taken. For instance, a course in algebra is often a prerequisite for a course in geometry.

private school: A school that is privately owned, rather than operated by a governmental department.

proctor: A person who supervises the taking of an examination to be certain there is no cheating, and that other rules are followed. Many nontraditional schools permit unproctored examinations.

professional school: School in which one studies for the various professions, including medicine, dentistry, law, nursing, veterinary, optometry, ministry, etc.

PSAT: Preliminary Scholastic Aptitude Test, given annually to high-school juniors.

public school: In the U.S., a school operated by the government of a city, county, district, state, or the federal government. In England, a privately owned or run school.

quarter: An academic term at a school on the "quarter system," in which the calendar year is divided into four equal quarters. New courses begin each quarter.

quarter hour: An amount of credit earned for each classroom hour spent in a given course during a given quarter. A course that meets four hours each week for a quarter would probably be worth four quarter hours, or quarter units.

recognized: A term used by some schools to indicate approval from some other organization or governmental body. The term usually does not have a precise meaning, so it may mean different things in different places.

registrar: The official at most colleges and universities who is responsible for maintaining student records and, in many cases, for verifying and validating applications for admission.

rolling admissions: A year-round admissions procedure. Many schools only admit students once or twice a year. A school with rolling admissions considers each application at the time it is received. Many nontraditional schools, especially ones with nonresident programs, have rolling admissions.

SAT: Scholastic Aptitude Test, one of the standard tests given to qualify for admission to colleges and universities.

scholarship: A study grant, either in cash or in the form of tuition or fee reduction.

score: Numerical rating of performance on a test. ("His score on the Graduate Record Exam was not so good.")

semester: A school term, generally four to five months. Schools on the semester system will usually have two semesters a year, with a shorter summer session.

semester hour: An amount of credit earned in a course representing one classroom hour per week for a semester. A class that meets three days a week for one hour, or one day a week for three hours, would be worth three semester hours, or semester units.

seminar: A form of instruction combining independent research with meetings of small groups of students and a faculty member, generally to report on reading or research the students have done.

senior: The fourth year of study of a four-year U.S. Bachelor's degree program, or a member of that class. ("Linnea is a senior this year, and is president of the senior class.")

sophomore: The second year of study in a four-year U.S. Bachelor's degree program, or a member of that class.

sorority: A women's social organization, often with its own living quarters on or near a campus, and usually identified with two or three Greek letters, such as Sigma Chi.

special education: Education of the physically or mentally handicapped, or, often, of the gifted.

special student: A student who is not studying for a degree either because he or she is ineligible or does not wish the degree.

statement of purpose: A detailed description of the career the applicant intends to pursue after graduation. A statement of purpose is often requested as part of the admissions procedure at a university.

subject: An area of study or learning covering a single topic, such as the subject of chemistry, or economics, or French literature.

subjective test: An examination in which the answers are in the form of narrative sentences or long or short essays, often expressing opinions rather than reporting facts.

syllabus: A detailed description of a course of study, often including the books to be read, papers to be written, and examinations to be given.

thesis: The major piece of research that is completed by many Master's degree candidates. A thesis is expected to show a detailed knowledge of one's field and ability to do research and integrate knowledge of the field.

TOEFL: Test of English as a Foreign Language, required by many schools of persons for whom English is not their native language.

traditional education: Education at a residential school in which the Bachelor's degree is completed through four years of classroom study, the Master's in one or two years, and the Doctorate in three to five years.

transcript: A certified copy of the student's academic record, showing courses taken, examinations passed, credits awarded, and grades or scores received.

transfer student: A student who has earned credit in one school, and then transfers to another school.

trimester: A term consisting of one third of an academic year. Some schools have three equal trimesters each year.

tuition: In the U.S., the money charged for formal instruction. In some schools, tuition is the only expense other than postage. In other schools, there may be fees as well as tuition. In England, tuition refers to the instruction or teaching at a school, such as the tuition offered in history.

tuition waiver: A form of financial assistance in which the school charges little or no tuition.

tutor: See *mentor*. A tutor can also be a hired assistant who helps a student prepare for a given class or examination.

undergraduate: Pertaining to the period of study from the end of high school to the earning of a Bachelor's degree; also to a person in such a course of study. ("Barry is an undergraduate at Reed College, one of the leading undergraduate schools.")

university: An institution that usually comprises one or more undergraduate colleges, one or more graduate schools, and, often, one or more professional schools.

Appendix I
Index To My Other Book

AS I EXPLAINED in appendix D, there are, of course, a great many more schools offering "alternative" or "nontraditional" approaches to earning degrees than the hundred in this book and the fifty more in appendix D. If you wish to learn more about a school not in this book, it may be in my *other* book on this topic, which offers much shorter descriptions on more than one thousand schools, good and bad. That book, *Bear's Guide to Earning College Degrees Non-Traditionally,* is available only by mail from F. & K. Costedoat, Box 826-T, Benicia, CA 94510. They will be glad to send you a free sixteen-page booklet telling about the book. To help you decide whether it might be of interest to you, here, with apologies for the very small type, is a copy of the index to *that other book:*

Index to This Book

R

Rapid Results College (England), 146, 148
Reading, as creditworthy life experience, 46
Recreation, as creditworthy life experience, 46
Red Cross, credit for training, 47
Reddeck, Edward, 173, 176
Referral service. See National Association for
    Private Post-Secondary Education
Regents College. See University of the State
    of New York
Regents Credit Bank, 42, 53-54
Regents External Degree—College Profi-
    ciency Programs, 39
Regis College (Colorado), **126**
Reid College of Detection Deception (Illi-
    nois), 176
Reuter, Dr. George, 27
Rhode Island, state accreditation agency for,
    17
Robinson, Delmer, 175
Roger Williams College (Rhode Island), **127**
Roosevelt University (Illinois), 34
Rules, flexibility in, 181-82
Rural Development Leadership Network, 60

S

Saginaw Valley State University, 82
St. David's University College (Wales), 156
Saint Edward's University (Texas), **128**
St. Giles University College, 176
Saint John's University (Louisiana), 176
Saint Joseph's College (Maine), 34, **129**
Saint-Mary-of-the-Woods College (Indiana),
    130
SAT. See Scholastic Aptitude Test
Savannah State College (Georgia), 34
Saybrook Institute (California), **131**
Scholastic Aptitude Test (SAT), 22
School Without a Name (Hawaii), 132
Schools
    checking out, 13-17
    information on additional, 169
    offering correspondence courses (list), 32-
        37
    offerings of, 19. See also Courses offered
Scoring, of CLEP and PEP examinations, 41
Scotland, schools in, 95, 173
Self-Assessment and Planning Manual, 47
Sheldrick, Dr. Reg, 136
Skidmore College (New York), **133**
Smithsonian Institution, 60
Somerset University (Louisiana and England),
    176
South Association of Colleges and Schools, 26
South Carolina, state accreditation agency for,
    17
South Dakota, state accreditation agency for,
    17
Southeastern College of the Assemblies of
    God (Florida), 34, **134**

Southern California University for Profes-
    sional Studies, **135**
Southern Illinois University, 34
Southland University, 27, 175
Southwest Texas State University, 34
Southwest University (Louisiana), **136**
Southwestern Adventist College (Texas), **137**
Southwestern University (Arizona), 176
Stanley H. Kaplan Educational Centers, 42
State agencies, and the legitimacy of schools,
    14-17
State University of Florida, **138**
State University of New York, 85
Stephens College (Missouri), **139**
Subjects
    of CLEP examinations, 40
    of PEP examinations, 40-41
Summit University (California, Idaho), 140
Summit University (Louisiana), **140**
SURGE program. See Colorado State Univer-
    sity
Sussex College of Technology (England), 176
Syracuse University (New York), **141**

T

Television
    courses offered on, 112, 113
    viewing, as creditworthy life experience, 46
Tennessee, state accreditation agency for, 17
Test, achievement, 22
Texas, state accreditation agency for, 17
Texas Tech University, 34
Theological University of America. See Univer-
    sity of America
Thomas Edison State College (New Jersey),
    75, 82, **142**, 155
Thomas University, 28
Time required
    for application procedure, 20
    for correspondence courses, 32
Travel, as creditworthy life experience, 46
Troy State University (Alabama), **143**

U

Union for Experimenting Colleges and Univer-
    sities, 144
Union Graduate School. See Union Institute
Union Institute (Ohio), 72, **144**
UNISA. See University of South Africa
United States University of America, 28
Universal Life Church, 27
Universal Life University (California), 177
Universidad Nacional Federico Villarreal
    (Peru), 161
University College of North Wales, 156
University College of Swansea (Wales), 156
University College of Wales, 156
University de la Romande (England), 177
University of Alabama, 34, **145**

University of Alaska, 34
University of America (Louisiana), 177
University of Arizona, 34
University of Arkansas, 35
University of Beverly Hills (Iowa), 177
University of California Extension, 35
University of Cincinnati, 119
University of Colorado, 35
University of Durham (England), **146**
University of East Georgia, 177
University of England, 177
University of Florida, 35, 138
University of Georgia, 35
University of Idaho, 35
University of Illinois, 35, 82
University of Iowa, 35, **147**
University of Kansas, 35
University of Kentucky, 35
University of London (England), **148**
University of Maryland, **149**
    University College, 119
University of Michigan, 35
University of Minnesota, 35
University of Mississippi, 35
University of Missouri, 35
    at Columbia, **150**
University of Nebraska, 36
University of Nevada, 36
University of New Mexico, 36
University of North America (Missouri), 173,
    177. See also North American Univer-
    sity
University of North Carolina, 36, 43
University of North Dakota, 36
University of North Florida, 138
University of Northern Colorado, 36
University of Northern Iowa, 36, 147
University of Oklahoma, 36, **151**
University of Phoenix (Arizona), 177
University of San Francisco (California), 82
University of Santa Barbara (California), **152**,
    153
University of Santa Monica (California), 177
University of Sarasota (Florida), **153**
University of South Africa (UNISA), **154**
University of South Carolina, 36
University of South Dakota, 36
University of South Florida, 40, 138
University of Southampton (England), 86
University of Southern Mississippi, 36
University of the State of New York, 47, 75,
    85, **155**
    Regents College, 42, 82
University of Tennessee, 36
University of Texas, 36
University of Utah, 37
University of Wales, **156**
    College of Cardiff, 156
University of Warwick (England), 146, **157**
University of Washington, 37
University of Waterloo (Canada), **158**
University of Wisconsin, 37

Other books by John Bear:

Finding Money for College
More than six and a half billion dollars in student loans goes unclaimed each year. This book shows how to find out about and use those specialized and general loans, as well as money from private foundations, grants, and creative, nontraditional ways to fund an education.
$6.95 paper, 168 pages

Computer Wimp
"If you're thinking about buying a computer or trashing the one you've got, read this book first"—*Personal Computing*
Dr. Bear believes that driving a computer should be as easy as driving a car—but, unfortunately, it rarely is. This witty, fact-filled book helps to change that situation, with hints on buying, using, and servicing your home or small-business computer.
$9.95 paper, 296 pages

How to Repair Food
with Marina Bear
Instead of throwing out that culinary disaster, you can repair it. Whether it's a fallen cake, salty soup, burned stew, overcooked broccoli, or any of hundreds of other unsavory mistakes, this book can help. "The greatest lift comes from the authors' encouraging, soothing tone: they combine the practicality of Heloise with the humor of Dr. Ruth." — *Publisher's Weekly*
$5.95 paper, 224 pages

Morning Food
with Margaret Fox
A wonderful book of breakfast and brunch foods from the nationally known Cafe Beaujolais. Includes muffins, breads, omelettes, and sinful coffee cakes, as well as less traditional fare such as breakfast soups, salads, and pastas. "...125 inviting recipes, amusing anecdotes, intelligent comments, and helpful kitchen tips..."—*Cookbook Digest*
$19.95 cloth, 208 pages

Cafe Beaujolais
with Margaret Fox
From a beautiful little restaurant in Northern California, a book celebrating fresh ingredients, great food, and country living. In addition to the 132 delicious recipes, CAFE BEAUJOLAIS offers hints and stories for anyone who's considered starting a restaurant. "If there's a better brunch to be found anywhere, I've never come close . . . Wonderful and innovative. But the genius of Margaret Fox is that the simplest breakfast dish comes out tasting like nothing you've ever experienced before."—Stan Sesser, *San Francisco Chronicle*
$12.95 paper or $19.95 cloth, 224 pages

Available from your local bookstore, or order direct from the publisher. Please include $1.25 shipping & handling for the first book, and 50 cents for each additional book. California residents include local sales tax. Write for our free complete catalog of over 400 books and tapes.

TEN SPEED PRESS Box 7123 Berkeley, California 94707